AF680497

Polis & Praxis Press

Contents

Introduction

Regarding social interaction, social circles tend to form as complex webs of relationships made of closeness, trust, and shared experiences. There is, however, a paradoxical truth here: the allure of large networks can hide the deep richness that can be found in a small, close-knit circle. As you move through this book I'm going to encourage you to throw out the common belief that big groups and quick acquaintances are good things. Let's instead engage in critical inquiry, where we challenge the assumptions that govern our perceptions of social interaction and explore the multifaceted nature of human relationships (or, in other words, let's discuss the notion that we're just playing along with a system that's no longer serving us).

The idea that language and meaning are inherently unreliable will come up frequently in this book. Words, signs, and body language are not fixed things; they are places where people argue and negotiate, and the conversations that happen around them shape them. Similarly, social circles are not fixed things; they form and change as power and desire change. We are freed from the limits of fixed identities and set social roles when we accept this fluidity. This makes it possible for us to make deeper, more genuine connections with other people. No need to force a thing if we understand its nature is to be fluid anyway.

I think it would be beneficial to you if we spent time in this book looking at how power works in social circles. Power isn't simply making people do what you want in a relationship. It's a bit more subtle and nuanced than that. In social groups, power dynamics determine who is included and who is left out. They choose who gets to be a part of the group and who gets pushed to the edges. We can find the hidden hierarchies that affect how we interact with each other by asking questions about these power dynamics. This forces us to deal with the unfair advantages and disadvantages that are a part of our daily lives. Here, we remember Nietzsche's "Will to Power," which says that power isn't just dominance but also making your own will and desires known in social situations. This idea makes us think about how people in the same social circle compete for power and control, changing the dynamics of who is included and who is excluded in small but significant ways.

Also, just a little self-reflection forces us to think about how language and conversation affect how we see the world. Language is performative, which means that it shapes our social identities and makes us feel like we have to act and play certain roles in order to fit in with what society expects of us. We can make room for new ways of interacting with each other that don't fit into neat categories by questioning everything we're supposed to believe about how we should *get along*.

When we think about social circles, it's smart to use the ideas of the Stoics as a possible framework. Stoicism, which stresses being self-aware, strong, and, for the most part, accepting of the way things are, can teach us a lot about how to build meaningful relationships. Stoicism teaches us to pay attention to what we can change—our thoughts, actions, and attitudes—rather than dwelling on outside events or other people's opinions. Stoic principles can help us deal with other people without needing their approval or validation. This lets us approach our relationships with calm and a sense of detachment.

The idea of stoicism also tells us to be thankful for the relationships we already have instead of always trying to make new ones. If we follow the idea that "virtue is the only good," we can put more value on the quality of our connections than the number of them. This is because we know that true happiness comes from having deep, meaningful relationships with a few people rather than many shallow connections with many people.

As you move through the rest of this book I want to encourage you to let go of the false ideas of stability and certainty that have possibly long shaped how you have thought about how you interact with others. Let's instead accept the ambiguity and complexity that make up the human experience. We should also be aware that our social circles are not fixed things, but rather fluid structures that change as power, desire, and conversation do. In the next few pages, we'll talk about how having a small, close-knit group of friends can change your life. We'll do this by taking a critical look at power dynamics, language, and identity, using the timeless wisdom of Stoicism to guide us. By asking these questions, we will find new ways to connect with others in a deeper, more genuine way, going beyond the limits of traditional social norms to embrace the fluidity and complexity of human relationships.

Chapter 1
Understanding Social Dynamics

"A friend is, as it were, a second self."
Marcus Tullius Cicero

When we look into the science behind social networks, we start to see how the complex web of human connections shapes our daily lives. As complicated webs of connections and interactions, social networks don't fit neatly into simple categories or can be explained in a straight line. Instead, they show up as changing events that are affected by many things, from the actions of individuals to the structure of society.

At the heart of our research is the idea that everything is connected, which is similar to the post-structuralist idea of relationality. Social networks are not separate things; they are hubs in bigger webs of social relationships, where people are connected through family, friendship, and membership. Patterns of clustering and homophily, the tendency for people to seek out or be attracted to those who are similar to themselves, can be seen in these networks. But within these clusters are bridges that link different groups and make it easier for information and ideas to move between different social spheres.

Different fields, like sociology, psychology, and network science, have a lot to teach us about social networks. Researchers use computers and statistics to make maps of the structure of social networks. These maps show how people are connected and help researchers find the most important people in these networks. The way people interact with each other is shaped by power dynamics, and these studies show how central actors and gatekeepers control the flow of resources and information.

In addition, social networks have properties that appear out of nowhere and are bigger than the sum of their parts. As the nodes in these networks talk to each other, new patterns of behavior and group outcomes appear. This is what causes things like social contagion and information cascades. These changes show how individual choice and social structure interact, which goes against ideas that social behavior is predetermined and shows how important context is in shaping how people interact with each other.

When we look at the science behind social networks, we see how complicated and unpredictable human relationships are. Networks are not fixed things; they are ongoing systems that change as people's tastes, social norms, and the condition of the environment do. Accepting this complexity can help us learn more about the rules that govern our social interactions, which will allow us to use social networks more wisely and critically.

Stoic philosopher Epictetus said, "Don't seek for everything to happen as you wish it would, but rather wish that everything happens as it actually will—then your life will flow well." Stoicism, which tells us to accept things as they are and focus on what we can change, can help us figure out how to use social networks more effectively. Realizing that everything is connected and practicing calmness in the face of uncertainty can help us be more resilient and clear in our interactions in social networks. Stoic ideas, like focusing on our own actions and intentions instead of what other people do or how they act, can help us handle the complicated world of social interactions with grace and humility.

Quality vs. Quantity: Debunking the Myth of Large Networks

The allure of big social networks often overshadows the value of close, meaningful connections in our always-connected world. But there is a basic truth that lies beneath the surface: the quality of our relationships is much more important than the number of connections we have. This difference between quality and quantity is at the heart of how we understand social dynamics. It forces us to rethink our priorities and what social capital really is.

Larger networks don't always mean more social support or emotional fulfillment, despite what most people think. In fact, studies have shown that the number of friends someone has is not strongly related to their happiness or satisfaction with their life. What makes us happy and makes us feel like we belong is not how many people we know or how close those relationships are.

The idea that quality is more important than quantity is also present in post-structuralist philosophy (a framework used throughout this book), which values deep human connections over shallow ones. Post-structuralism breaks down fixed ideas of identity and social roles. It encourages us to build relationships based on authenticity and mutual understanding, not just being close or convenient. By putting the quality of our connections first, we can build meaningful connections that make our lives better and give us a sense of belonging in a world that is becoming more and more divided.

Also, keeping up with the demands of a large social network can be mentally and emotionally draining, as we try to keep up with the demands of constant communication and social engagement. An interesting phenomenon called "network fatigue" shows how having a lot of friends can hurt our mental and emotional health, causing us to feel overwhelmed and burned out.

Smaller, more personal social circles, on the other hand, provide a safe space of support and understanding where people can be themselves without worrying about being judged or rejected. People in these close-knit groups feel like they belong and are connected in a way that larger, less personal networks don't always provide. We can build a support system that helps us through life's challenges and celebrates our successes by putting time and effort into building deep, meaningful relationships.

The myth of large networks comes from the wrong idea that being popular and high on the social ladder means you are happy and fulfilled. In reality, what makes us truly happy is not how many connections we have, but how well we care for and cherish the ones we have. By focusing on quality over quantity, we can build a web of connections that make our lives better and give us a sense of purpose and belonging in a world that is becoming more complicated and confusing.

Stoicism can help us figure out how to deal with complicated social situations and put quality over quantity in our relationships. We can be happier and more fulfilled in our social interactions if we follow stoic principles like focusing on what we can control and being thankful for the relationships we already have. Stoic practices like writing in a journal, reflecting, and practicing mindfulness can help us connect with others in a deeper, more meaningful way. This can help us feel like we belong and are connected in a way that goes beyond the shallowness of large social networks.

The Psychology of Close Relationships

The most important thing about human relationships is that they provide an opportunity for intimate connections, or experiencing *closeness* to another human being. Bonds of trust and closeness are what make connections meaningful. The psychology of close relationships looks into the complicated dynamics that shape how we interact with the people we care about the most. It sheds light on the difficulties of love, attachment, and simply talking to other people.

Attachment theory is a central idea in our understanding of close relationships. It says that our early experiences with caregivers shape how we think about relationships, which in turn shapes how we attach and become intimate with others throughout our lives. Attachment theory, which is based on psychoanalysis and developmental psychology, stresses how important secure attachments are for building emotional strength and mental health.

The psychology of close relationships also looks at how empathy and emotional intelligence can help people get closer and feel more connected. Being able to understand and share other people's feelings is called empathy. It's an important part of healthy relationships because it helps people understand each other's needs and respond with kindness and care. Being emotionally intelligent, which includes knowing yourself, being able to control your emotions, and having good social skills, is very important for getting along with others and solving problems in a healthy way.

Close relationships also have patterns of how people talk to each other and interact that shape the emotional climate of the relationship. Gottman's research on marriage stability shows how important positive communication styles like active listening, empathy, and validation are for building trust and closeness between partners. On the other hand, negative communication patterns like criticism, defensiveness, and contempt can tear a relationship apart, making both people feel angry and disconnected.

As we look into the psychology of close relationships, we are reminded of how weak and fragile human connections are. People in close relationships have to put in time and effort to keep them going as they go through the ups and downs of closeness and distance, love and conflict. Understanding the psychological dynamics that support our closest relationships can help us develop more empathy, better communication skills, and emotional strength. This can help us build stronger, more fulfilling relationships with the people we care about.

Stoicism has a lot to teach us about how to handle the difficulties of close relationships with grace and strength (and you'll find that this book is littered with quotes and lessons from the likes of Seneca, Epictetus, Marcus Aurelius, Cicero, and Socrates). Focusing on what we can control and accepting that things outside of our control will change over time are stoic principles that can help us deal with our relationships with loved ones with peace and acceptance. Stoic practices like writing in a journal, thinking about things, and being mindful can help us become more self-aware and control our emotions, which can help us handle problems in our relationships with wisdom and grace.

To learn more about the psychology of close relationships, it's important to look into the different attachment styles that attachment theory describes. These attachment styles, such as secure, anxious, and avoidant attachment, affect how people feel and react to closeness and intimacy in relationships. Learning about attachment styles can help you understand how relationships work and give you useful information about the problems and chances for growth in close relationships.

Also, looking into the part that emotional closeness plays in long-term relationships can help us learn more about what makes relationships happy and last. Sharing your thoughts, feelings, and weaknesses with a trusted partner creates emotional intimacy and a sense of closeness and connection that goes beyond being close. Emotional intimacy requires people to be open, vulnerable, and trust each other as they interact with each other and figure out how to share personal information and show empathy.

Additionally, the psychology of close relationships includes the study of ways to keep and fix relationships. Researchers have found a number of behaviors and ways of talking to each other that make relationships more stable and satisfying. These include actively listening, showing appreciation, and working together to solve problems. People can strengthen the bonds of closeness and trust in their close relationships by using these relationship-enhancing strategies. This will make both partners feel safer and better.

Looking into how technology affects close relationships can teach us a lot about how digital tools for communication change the dynamics of closeness and connection. More and more people are finding it hard to keep close relationships in the digital age, thanks to the rise of social media and other online communication tools. Figuring out the pros and cons of using technology in close relationships can help you come up with better ways to talk to each other, get closer, and avoid problems that might come up when you're online.

When we think about the psychology of close relationships, it's important to think about how cultural and societal factors affect how we see and feel about closeness and connection. Cultural norms, gender roles, and societal expectations affect how people approach and handle close relationships. These factors affect how people talk to each other, how relationships work, and how they show they are close. When we look at how culture and psychology interact in close relationships, we can learn more about the different ways people experience and show love, attachment, and connection in different cultural settings.

Studying the psychology of close relationships gives us a deep and nuanced picture of how our closest relationships work. By learning more about attachment theory, emotional closeness, relationship maintenance strategies, and how technology and culture affect close relationships, we can get a better sense of what makes relationships happy and healthy. Stoic philosophy can help us deal with the difficulties of close relationships with wisdom, strength, and compassion, leading to deeper connections and greater happiness in our interactions with others.

5 Things to Consider

Choose Depth Over Breadth: When building your social networks, choose the quality and depth of your relationships over the number of people you connect with. Instead of making a lot of friends, focus on building close, meaningful relationships with a small group of people.

Know the Power of Small Circles: Know that small, close-knit social networks can provide more emotional support, understanding, and happiness than larger, less personal networks. Spend time and effort on these close relationships because they give you a sense of connection and belonging that is important for your health.

Accept Vulnerability and Authenticity: When you're close to someone, accept their vulnerability and authenticity as the basis for a deep connection. Being honest about your feelings, thoughts, and experiences with people you trust builds a sense of closeness and trust that makes the bond between people stronger.

Practice Mindful Communication: Mindful communication means paying attention to how you talk to people close to you and trying to develop good communication habits like active listening, empathy, and validation. Avoid negative communication patterns that hurt trust and closeness. Instead, try to communicate in a way that builds mutual respect and understanding.

Draw Wisdom from Stoic Philosophy: To handle the tricky situations in social situations with poise and strength, use what you've learned from stoic philosophy. Focusing on what you can control, being thankful for the relationships you already have, and putting virtue ahead of external outcomes are all stoic ideas that you should follow. If you follow stoic practices every day, you can make deeper, more meaningful connections with other people and get more out of your social interactions.

Reflection Questions

What qualities do I value most in my social connections, and how do these preferences shape the composition of my social network?

In what ways do I prioritize quantity over quality in my relationships, and how does this impact my overall sense of fulfillment and well-being?

How do I navigate the balance between vulnerability and authenticity in my close relationships, and what barriers do I encounter in expressing my true self?

What communication patterns do I observe within my close relationships, and how do these patterns contribute to or detract from feelings of intimacy and trust?

How can I incorporate principles from stoic philosophy into my approach to social dynamics, and what strategies can I implement to cultivate deeper, more meaningful connections with others?

Chapter 2

Assessing Your Current Social Circle

"Associate with people who are likely to improve you."
Seneca

Our social circles are fundamental in determining our experiences, emotions, and sense of self in our daily life. These circles are composed of varying degrees of connections, from the deeply intimate to the more casual. Maintaining our emotional well-being and building good, encouraging relationships depend on a process of understanding and assessing our social circles. This chapter explores the crucial task of evaluating your current social circle, guiding you through a reflective journey that encompasses identifying your core relationships, scrutinizing the dynamics within your circle, and recognizing the impact of toxic relationships.

Identifying Your Core Relationships

Starting with your core relationships will help you to grasp the architecture of your social circle. The depth of connection, trust, and mutual support these relationships reflect define them more than just proximity or frequency of interaction. This process is driven mostly by your need to define which relationships in your life have great importance and impact.

Think first of the people who are most important in your life. These are the people you turn to for emotional support, to share in your ups and downs, and with whom you really feel loyalty and trust. Think not only of family members or long-time friends but also of mentors, colleagues, or even more recent friends who have rapidly become essential to your psychological and emotional stability.

Finding these basic links calls for transcending traditional labels and categories. Rather than just enumerating people according to their position—that of family, friends, or colleagues—pay attention to the nature of your contact with them. Ask yourself things like: *In a crisis, who do I call? Who welcomes and understands me for exactly who I am? Who is someone that pushes me toward personal development and excellence?* These questions enable you to identify the actual nature of your main relationships.

Take also into account the reciprocity in these interactions. Real relationships are distinguished by a fair sharing of care and support. Think about if these interactions are one-sided or if they are mutually beneficial. Finding imbalances helps you to highlight the dynamics requiring change or attention.

This process also helps you realize how erratic relationships are. Although some relationships are fleeting, for a given period of your life they have great importance. Some might be long-standing but have changed in significance over time. Understanding this fluidity will help you value the dynamic character of your social circle and change your perspective of basic relationships.

Evaluating the Dynamics Within Your Circle

After your basic relationships have been identified, you should assess the dynamics in your social circle. This entails looking at how these relationships work, the part each person plays, and the underlying trends forming your interactions.

Look first at the power relations inside your circle. Power shows itself in more subdued forms including influence, support, and decision-making than it does only in overt control or dominance. Think about who is the emotional anchor, who most influences group decisions, and who usually plays a more subdued role. Knowing these dynamics will help you see how power and influence are balanced in your relationships—or not.

Then examine your circle's communication trends. Good relationships are mostly dependent on effective communication, which promotes understanding and connection. Think about how candidly and truthfully you and your key relationships interact. Do you know of anyone you could share your most personal ideas and emotions with without concern for criticism?

Take into account the emotional environment of your social circle. This covers your interactions' general tone and attitude. Do your relationships tend to be more negative, critical, or draining or are they marked by optimism, encouragement, and support? Your mental and emotional well-being can be heavily influenced by the emotional environment they create which can affect your perspective on all of your relationships, including the relationship you have with yourself.

It's also crucial to consider how limits fit into your social circle. Good relationships call for well defined, respected limits that let people keep their autonomy and promote closeness. Think about whether you and your key relationships have respected and set limits for one another. Are limits routinely crossed, causing discomfort or bitterness?

Evaluate the degree of dedication and financial support your key relationships demand or assume from you and one another. This includes thinking about the time, energy, and work you and your interactions invest in preserving and tending to these ties. Knowing your degree of dedication will help you spot relationships that might call for more thought or review.

Recognizing the Impact of Toxic Relationships

Often typified by patterns of manipulation, control, disrespect, and emotional harm, toxic relationships can be detrimental to your mental and emotional health.

Start by spotting the indicators of unhealthy relationships in your social circle. Consistent negative attitude, criticism, and lack of support can all be indicators here. Think back on relationships in which you often feel stressed, exhausted, or depressed. Are there people who regularly undercut your self-esteem, violate your boundaries, or start pointless drama and conflict?

Furthermore, an awareness of the subtle kinds of poison that might contaminate relationships is crucial. This can be comprised of emotional manipulation, guilt-tripping, and passive-aggressive behavior. Over time, these actions can erode your sense of self-worth and well-being.

Think about how these poisonous relationships affect your life in a general sense. Think about how they influence your self-esteem, mental and emotional health, and capacity for positive, supportive relationships. Toxic relationships can create a cloud of stress and anxiety that affects your capacity to concentrate, reach your objectives, and enjoy life.

Understanding toxic relationships also means considering your own part in these dynamics. Although you should recognize the damage others cause, introspection will help you see how you might be supporting or encouraging these negative behaviors. Examining your own actions, communication style, and limits in these relationships can help you to grow.

Identifying any poisonous relationships you're currently in comes first; then, you have to decide how to handle them. This can entail establishing and enforcing limits, asking for help from reliable friends or experts, and—in some situations—distancing yourself from or terminating the relationship. Although these actions can be difficult, leading a less stressed and more fulfilling life depends on giving your mental and emotional health top priority.

Stoicism provides insightful analysis of handling poisonous relationships. Seneca said, "Associate with people who are likely to improve you." This idea challenges us to surround ourselves with people who uplift and support us instead of those who drain and hurt us. Focusing on our own actions, reactions, and decisions helps us to negotiate negative relationships with more resilience and wisdom.

Evaluating your current social circle ultimately requires a thorough review of your core relationships, the dynamics within your circle, and the effects of negative relationships. You can create a social circle that supports and enhances your life by spotting and fostering significant relationships, assessing the roles and patterns in your relationships, and resolving negative dynamics. Adopting stoic ideas will help you to stay resilient, clear, and purposeful in your social interactions as well as guide you in this process.

5 Things to Consider

Identify Core Relationships: Reflect on which relationships in your life provide the most emotional support, trust, and mutual growth. Prioritize these relationships since they define your social circle and greatly affect your quality of life.

Evaluate Relationship Dynamics: Review the power dynamics, communication styles, and emotional climates in your social circle. Knowing these elements will enable you to create better relationships, set reasonable limits, and make sure your interactions are respectful and balanced.

Recognize and Address Toxicity: Acknowledge and deal with toxic relationships that sap your energy, undercut your self-esteem, or cause emotional pain. Maintaining your mental and emotional health requires you to develop plans to either distance yourself from or dissolve these negative relationships.

Foster Emotional Intelligence and Empathy: Encourage the people you know to increase their emotional intelligence and empathy. These traits are crucial for knowing and sympathetically addressing the needs of others.

Incorporate Stoic Principles: Accept Stoic ideas to negotiate the complexity of social interactions with wisdom and fortitude. While learning acceptance and equanimity in the face of outside events, pay close attention to what is within your control—your own actions and reactions. This strategy can enable you to create closer and more supportive relationships.

Reflection Questions

Who are the core individuals in my life that I turn to for emotional support, trust, and mutual growth? How do these relationships positively impact my well-being?

What are the power dynamics and communication patterns within my social circle? Are these dynamics balanced, and do they promote healthy, respectful interactions?

Are there any relationships in my social circle that consistently drain my energy or cause emotional distress? How can I address these toxic dynamics to protect my mental and emotional health?

How can I improve my emotional intelligence and empathy in my interactions with others? What specific actions can I take to better understand and respond to the needs of those in my core relationships?

How can I incorporate Stoic principles, such as focusing on what is within my control and practicing acceptance, into my approach to social interactions? In what ways can these principles help me build more meaningful and supportive relationships?

Chapter 3
Setting Boundaries

"We are not privy to the stories behind people's actions, so we should be patient with others and suspend judgment of them, recognizing the limits of our understanding."
Epictetus

Setting boundaries is a necessary but sometimes disregarded habit when it comes to developing new friendships and relationships. Boundaries guide our interactions and relationships by defining our personal space, autonomy, and values—that is, by establishing invisible lines that typically only we are aware of. Acting as a shield, they protect our mental, emotional, and physical health. But the skill of setting and preserving these limits is rife with difficulties, misunderstandings, and confusion. This chapter explores the several dimensions of boundary-setting and provides a thorough manual for negotiating this important component of personal dynamics.

The Art of Saying "No"

Saying "no" is a basic yet sometimes difficult part of establishing limits. It announces one's limits, tastes, and autonomy. Saying "no" is difficult for many people because of cultural standards, society expectations, and internalized conflicts or rejection concerns. Still, keeping personal integrity and well-being depends on mastery of this art.

Saying "no" can be challenging mostly because one worries about disappointing others. Many people are taught to put the needs and wants of others above their own, which results in a widespread guilt when one declines demands.

One must first realize the need of "no," if one is to start recovering its power. Saying "no" is a necessary element of self-care and respect, not a sign of selfishness or rebellion. It helps people guard their time, energy, and resources so as to prevent overuse or exploitation. Setting limits helps you create an environment free from the resentment and burnout sometimes associated with overcommitting so that real connections and interactions may develop.

Saying "no" calls on a change of viewpoint. It should be understood as a positive confirmation of one's values and priorities rather than a negative or confrontational act. This reframe helps people overcome the guilt and anxiety sometimes connected with rejection, enabling them to boldly assert their limitations.

Furthermore, one has to create plans for properly saying "no." One way is to communicate clearly and succinctly. Ambiguity can cause misinterpretation and repeated demands, making future interactions awkward or unpleasant. Giving a quick justification will also help communicate the sincerity and firmness of your stance without resorting to overly dramatic apologies or justification.

To boost confidence, one can also learn to say "no" in less important events. Role-playing situations with a friend you trust or thinking back on past events where saying "no" would have been helpful helps people be ready for real-life interactions. This exercise can help you realize that saying "no" is a talent that you can acquire and improve over time.

Saying "no" is really about recovering one's agency and claiming the right to give personal well-being top priority. Laying the groundwork for better and more balanced relationships, it promotes respect—from inside oneself as much as from others.

Finding Appropriate Restraints

Setting boundaries depends on establishing reasonable limits, which define the boundaries of acceptable behavior and interactions. These boundaries help to preserve your mental, emotional, and physical well-being by guiding what you are ready to accept and participate in.

The first step in establishing reasonable boundaries is self-awareness. Determining what limits are required depends on you knowing your needs, values, and triggers. This introspection entails thinking back on past events when limits were either honored or broken and considering how these events affected your welfare.

Healthy limits are personal by nature and vary greatly between one person and another. One person might, for example, need more alone time to recover, while another might give social events top priority. Setting reasonable and sustainable boundaries depends on an awareness of and respect for these unique characteristics.

Starting with small, reasonable limits and progressively extending them as necessary is one great way to establish good limits. This slow process helps people to become confident in their capacity to set boundaries and change their limits depending on comments and experience. One might start, for instance, by defining a limit around work-related correspondence outside of business hours and then progressively set limits in other spheres of life.

Consistency is still another crucial component of setting reasonable limits. Different approaches of enforcing limits might cause uncertainty and compromise their efficiency. Consistent communication and upholding of limits help to underline their relevance and show a dedication to self-respect and well-being.

Establishing reasonable limits also requires, when needed, negotiation and compromise. Declaring one's limits is crucial, but equally so is keeping an eye on the needs and viewpoints of others. Striking a balance between rigidity and adaptability will help to preserve good relationships and guard personal welfare.

Within personal relationships, setting reasonable boundaries calls for honest and open communication. Talking about limits with others can help to define expectations and avoid misinterpretation. Approaching these conversations with empathy and respect helps to show that boundary-setting is a mutual process that benefits all the participants.

Using stoic philosophy helps one to improve the habit of setting reasonable boundaries. Understanding that we have no influence over the behavior or responses of others helps us to concentrate on claiming and maintaining our own limits with composure and clarity.

Ultimately, establishing reasonable limits calls for self-awareness, consistency, and good communication—all of which depend on one another. Understanding and respecting our own needs and values will help us to establish limits that support good, balanced relationships and safeguard our well-being.

Appropriate Boundary Communication

The foundation of boundary-setting is good communication. It entails being open to others' limits and clearly and forcefully expressing one's own to them. The aim is to foster good interactions and relationships by means of a mutual understanding and respect.

Establishing limits starts with clarity. Statements that are vague or ambiguous can cause misinterpretation and compromise the efficacy of the boundary. When expressing one's constraints, one should be direct and exact. Saying, *"I need some space,"* for instance, might be replaced by, *"I need an hour of quiet time after work to unwind."*

Boundary communication also depends on timing. The result of the conversation can be changed by deciding when to talk about boundaries. Usually, it is better to handle limits in a cool, nonjudging environment than in the heat of the moment. Choosing the appropriate moment and strategy can benefit from preparation for the discussion and consideration of the viewpoint of the other person.

Assertiveness is also important for good boundary communication. Being assertive is respectfully and confidently expressing one's needs and constraints, free from passivity or aggression. It's about honoring the limits of others while yet firmly staying within one's own. By emphasizing on one's own feelings and needs instead of blaming or criticizing the other person, "I" statements can help to enable assertive communication. For instance, *"I get overwhelmed when I get late night work emails. I have to restrict office hours of work communications to a certain window of time."*

In boundary communication, active listening is also vital. It entails trying to grasp the other person's viewpoint, validating their emotions, and paying attention to their response. This reciprocal approach helps to build mutual respect and cooperation, facilitating boundary maintenance and negotiation. Open-ended questions and summaries of the other person's comments help to show active listening and advance positive communication.

When establishing limits, you should also expect and control possible pushback. Some people might object to the limits being imposed either because they are not used to them or because they believe their own needs are being compromised. While addressing the other person's concerns, responding to pushback with empathy and firmness can help strengthen the boundary. For instance, appreciating their emotions and restating the value of the boundary will help to validate their viewpoint while yet preserving the boundary.

Drawing on stoic philosophy, emphasizing what is within our control helps us to practice good boundary communication. It motivates us to build relationships based on mutual respect and support whereby limits are appreciated and maintained. Regardless of the answers we get, by concentrating on our own actions and reactions we can clearly and confidently express our limits.

Properly communicating limits calls for clarity, assertiveness, attentive listening, and handling pushback. Respectful and sympathetic approach of boundary talks will help to establish mutual understanding that promotes balanced relationships. Combining stoic philosophy's insights will help us to better convey limits with wisdom and resilience, guaranteeing respectful and empowering interactions.

5 Things to Consider

Understanding the Importance of "No": Acknowledge that establishing boundaries depends on saying "no". It's a required step in safeguarding your time, energy, and well-being, not a show of rebellion or self-serving behavior. Think back on times when declining could have kept your limits intact and avoided burnout or resentment.

Self-Awareness and Reflection: Take some time to consider your own needs, values, and emotional triggers. Establishing reasonable boundaries requires this self-awareness. Think back on past events when your boundaries were honored or violated and how those events shaped you. These reflections will help you to define reasonable limits that fit your own level of well-being.

Effective Communication Strategies: To express your limits, hone strong, clear, assertive communication techniques. Use "I" statements to communicate your needs and emotions without assigning blame or criticism to others. To help to prevent misunderstandings in your conversations, be clear and direct. When talking about limits, keep in mind context and timing are crucial.

Managing Pushback and Resistance: When you set or enforce limits, expect some people to object. Get ready to answer opposition with empathy and tenacity. Though everyone will not accept your limits right away, stay consistent and polite to help them become stronger with time.

Incorporating Stoic Principles: Apply stoic philosophy's ideas to your methods of setting limits. Rather than trying to influence others' reactions, concentrate on what you can control—your actions, answers, and choices. Welcome Seneca's wisdom: "Associate with people who are likely to improve you." Surround yourself with people who respect and support your limits since this will help you to keep them rather easily.

Reflection Questions

How comfortable am I with saying "no" to requests that overextend me or compromise my values? What internal or external factors contribute to my difficulty in saying "no"?

What specific needs, values, and triggers have I identified in myself that require the establishment of clear boundaries? How have past experiences of boundary violations impacted my well-being, and what patterns can I recognize?

In what ways can I improve my communication skills to effectively convey my boundaries? How can I use "I" statements and specific language to express my needs without causing conflict or misunderstanding?

How do I typically respond to pushback or resistance when I set boundaries? What strategies can I implement to manage these challenges while maintaining my boundaries with empathy and firmness?

How can I incorporate stoic principles into my approach to boundary-setting? What aspects of stoic philosophy, such as focusing on what is within my control and seeking supportive relationships, can help me navigate the complexities of maintaining my boundaries?

Chapter 4
Cultivating Authentic Connections

"True happiness is... to enjoy the present, without anxious dependence upon the future." Seneca

Authentic connections are not merely transactions of words or gestures but profound exchanges of hearts and minds. They explore the depths of our shared humanity rather than following the flimsiness of social graces. Fundamentally, they are vulnerable—that is, ready to show our actual selves, flaws and all, in search of real connection. Accepting vulnerability is an assertion of our bravery to be seen, understood, and accepted for who we really are, not a sign of weakness. We yearn for connections that are deep and honest. This chapter explores the art of cultivating authentic connections while discussing the essence of vulnerability, trust, and meaningful communication.

Embracing Vulnerability

Developing real relationships is mostly dependent on the great and sometimes difficult act of embracing vulnerability. Vulnerability is a great monument to our humanity, not a weakness as society would have it. We expose our actual selves by means of vulnerability, revealing our hopes, worries, and fears. This transparency promotes closer, more real connections with people, enabling relationships to go beyond surface exchanges.

One must first acknowledge the psychological and cultural obstacles preventing the expression of vulnerability if one is to grasp it. Often valuing invulnerability, society defines strength as emotional stoicism combined with self-sufficiency. This cultural story exhorts people to hide their weaknesses, which results in relationships based more on appearances than on authenticity. Overcoming this cultural conditioning calls for a basic change in viewpoint—that vulnerability is not a sign of weakness but rather of courage and strength.

Being vulnerable starts with self-awareness. It calls for a readiness to face and grow used to our own flaws and fears. Real vulnerability is based on this self-acceptance since it lets us show ourselves really free from concern of rejection or criticism. Reflecting on past events where sensitivity was greeted with acceptance and understanding will help one to strengthen the good features of this practice and increase faith in its worth.

Moreover, vulnerability entails a conscious decision to let people see you. This decision exposes us to possible damage or rejection, thus it is naturally dangerous. Still, this risk helps to create deep relationships. Let others see our actual selves; then, we invite them to see the same, fostering a mutual understanding and empathy space. This reciprocity strengthens the bond and helps one feel intimate and belonging.

Drawing on stoic philosophy, we can discover more power in embracing fragility. Stoicism's emphasis on our internal reactions and the need of learning to accept events beyond our reach should be considered here. Accepting our weaknesses and the uncertainty of others' responses helps us to approach interactions with more peace and openness. "True happiness is... to enjoy the present, without anxious dependence upon the future," Seneca said. Accepting vulnerability is consistent with this idea since it means being real and present in our interactions without worrying too much about possible results.

Intentional activities help one to embrace vulnerability. Even in little increments, sharing personal stories and emotions helps one progressively feel more vulnerable. Furthermore, designing surroundings that support transparency—that is, safe, nonjudging environments—may help this practice to build and cause us to be comfortable enough to do it more.

Developing real relationships depends mostly on accepting vulnerability. It calls for self-awareness, bravery, and a readiness to walk emotional tightropes. Deeper, more significant relationships can be developed by changing our viewpoint to see vulnerability as a strength and using stoic techniques to control our worries. This habit improves not only our relationships with others but also our own psychological and emotional wellness.

Building Trust and Intimacy

Real connections are based on trust and intimacy, which are therefore fundamental elements of each other. Developing intimacy and trust calls both deliberate effort and consistent behavior as well as a dedication to mutual respect and understanding.

Fundamentally, trust is the conviction in the dependability, morality, and goodness of another person. It grows over time by regular behavior and open communication. One has to first show dependability in both minor and important issues to build confidence. This dependability lays the basis of confidence since it indicates that one can be relied upon in many different situations and that they are consistent.

Developing trust depends on honesty. This includes not only speaking honestly but also being open about one's goals, emotions, and restrictions. In relationships, honesty guarantees that interactions are based on reality rather than illusion, promoting a feeling of safety. It also promotes mutual honesty, fostering a dynamic in which both sides feel free to show their actual selves.

Developing trust also depends on empathy and attentive listening. We show others we value and respect them by really listening to them and validating their experiences and emotions. This validation shows a dedication to knowing and helping one another, strengthening trust. Particularly empathy helps us to connect on a deeper level since it requires not only knowledge of another's viewpoint but also sharing in their emotional experience.

Closely associated with trust, intimacy is a great sense of closeness and connection. It is distinguished by emotional sharing, mutual vulnerability, and an understanding and acceptance attitude. Developing intimacy calls for the readiness to communicate about one's inner world, sharing ideas, emotions, and experiences not usually exposed. This candor invites the other person to follow suit, fostering a reciprocal interaction that strengthens the bond.

Development of intimacy depends on both physical and emotional presence. Being present is giving undivided attention, totally participating in the moment, and expressing real interest in the other person. This presence shows dedication and compassion, strengthening the link and promoting a feeling of belonging.

Inspired by stoic philosophy, emphasizing moral behavior helps us develop trust and intimacy. Stoicism stresses the need of virtues including honesty, integrity, and compassion—qualities fundamental to trust and intimacy. Through modeling these qualities in our connections, we can build rapport based on mutual respect and understanding.

Moreover, stoicism emphasizes the need of paying attention to our actions and reactions, so influencing what we can control. This implies that, in the framework of developing intimacy and trust, we should be constant in our behavior, keep honesty and openness, and show compassion and concern. Emphasizing these elements will help us to build a solid basis for intimacy and trust independent of outside conditions.

Deliberate actions can help to build intimacy and trust. To improve these aspects, one should often participate in honest and open dialogues, show thanks and respect, and be consistent and reliable.

To develop real relationships, then, trust and intimacy are absolutely vital. It calls for dependability, integrity, empathy, and a dedication to mutual respect and comprehension. Drawing on stoic ideas and emphasizing moral behavior will help us improve our capacity to establish trust and intimacy, fostering relationships that are both significant and satisfying. These components help us maintain our emotional and psychological well-being as well as to deepen our relationships with others.

Fostering Meaningful Conversations

Real connections flow from meaningful conversations. They probe our deepest ideas, emotions, and experiences, transcending surface interactions. Building and preserving real relationships depends on understanding, empathy, and a feeling of connection that these talks help to develop.

One must first develop the skill of active listening if one is to encourage deep conversations. Active listening is really interacting with the speaker, paying close attention to their words, tone, and body language. It calls for letting go of distractions and preconceptions so that one may really live in the moment. Active listening helps us to demonstrate our respect of the other person's viewpoint and sincere desire in knowing their experience.

Important conversations depend on empathy. It entails not only grasping the viewpoint of the other person but also accompanying in their emotional experience. Empathy builds a link between people, promoting mutual understanding and connection. Mindfulness and self-awareness help us develop empathy since they improve our capacity to tune into the feelings and experiences of others.

One very effective tool for encouraging deep conversations is open-ended questions. Instead of offering simple yes-or-no responses, these questions invite the other person to offer more about their ideas, feelings, and experiences. Open-ended questions range in nature from *"What are your thoughts on this?"* or *"How did that experience make you feel?"*

Real meaningful conversations also depend on vulnerability. Sharing our own ideas, emotions, and experiences—especially those delicate or personal—invites the other person to follow suit. Deeper connections are made possible by this reciprocity, creating a space of mutual trust and openness. Remember that vulnerability is a decision and should be pursued in a way that seems reasonable and safe for both sides.

Meaningful conversations also call for a mix between listening and talking. Sharing our own viewpoint is vital, but equally so is allowing the other person to share theirs. This harmony guarantees that both sides feel heard and valuable and helps to build mutual respect.

Inspired by stoic philosophy, we can improve our capacity to create meaningful dialogues by concentrating on moral values including integrity, compassion, and awareness. Along with the need of honest and open communication, stoicism emphasizes the need of being present and sincerely involved in our conversations.

Deliberate activities can help to create meaningful conversations. Establishing a good environment free from distractions and fit for honest communication will help to set the stage for important interactions. Approach talks with a real interest in the other person's viewpoint instead of an agenda or preconceptions.

One can also get insightful analysis by looking back on earlier exchanges. Think about the exchanges that seemed especially significant and fulfilling—what made them so? What attitudes or actions added to the depth of the conversation? Reflecting on these events helps us to spot trends and behaviors that support meaningful conversations and implement them the next time we engage in conversation with that person or group.

To develop real connections, then, meaningful conversations are more important than ever. It calls for open-ended questions, empathy, active listening, vulnerability, and a mix between speaking and listening. Drawing on stoic ideas and emphasizing virtues like honesty and mindfulness will help us to improve our capacity to participate in meaningful conversations and interactions, building deep and satisfying relationships. These talks improve not only our relationships with others but also our own psychological and emotional wellness.

5 Things to Consider

Embracing Vulnerability: Think about how your relationship with vulnerability shapes your interactions with others. Think about the psychological and cultural barriers preventing vulnerability and look at ways to get beyond them. Accepting vulnerability lets you enter closer, more real relationships with people.

Building Trust and Intimacy: Review your relationships' degree of intimacy and trust and think about ways to improve these aspects. Think about how trust is developed from dependability, honesty, and empathy. Create surroundings that support vulnerability and openness so that you may develop closer relationships with people all around.

Fostering Meaningful Conversations: Evaluate the caliber of your interactions and think about ways to make them more significant and beneficial. To open a forum for more in-depth inquiry and understanding, practice active listening, empathy, and vulnerability. Create chances for connection and invite real conversation by using open-ended questions.

Exploring Stoic Principles: Examine stoic philosophy's insights and think about how they might improve your method of fostering real relationships. Think about moral qualities including mindfulness, honesty, and integrity and apply them in your interactions with others. Accept the idea of stressing what you can influence to strengthen your relationships and create closer bonds.

Practical Application and Reflection: Take practical steps to apply the principles discussed in this chapter to your daily interactions. In your relationships, create chances for vulnerability, trust-building, and deep dialogues. Think back on past events and talks to find behaviors that support real connections; then, apply these ideas to direct your next few interpersonal interactions.

Reflection Questions

How comfortable am I with embracing vulnerability in my relationships? What cultural or psychological barriers inhibit my ability to be vulnerable, and how can I overcome them to foster deeper connections with others?

What strategies do I currently employ to build trust and intimacy in my relationships? How can I enhance these strategies to create a stronger foundation for genuine connection and understanding?

In what ways do I approach conversations with others, and how do these approaches impact the depth and authenticity of our interactions? What steps can I take to foster more meaningful conversations that encourage vulnerability, empathy, and mutual understanding?

How can I integrate insights from stoic philosophy into my approach to cultivating authentic connections? How do virtues such as honesty, integrity, and mindfulness enhance the quality of my relationships, and how can I embody these virtues more fully in my interactions with others?

What practical steps can I take to apply the principles discussed in this chapter to my daily interactions? How can I create environments that encourage openness, trust, and vulnerability, and how can I reflect on past experiences to identify areas for growth and improvement in my relationships?

Chapter 5

Navigating Social Media and Technology

"This is the first promise that philosophy holds out to us: fellow-feeling, humanity, sociability."
Seneca

In the digital age, our lives are intricately intertwined with technology and social media, shaping the way we connect, communicate, and interact with one another. The various platforms we use (Facebook, Instagram, Reddit, TikTok, etc.) present hitherto unheard-of chances for networking, idea sharing, and keeping in touch with friends and loved ones all around the globe. Underneath the surface of digital connectivity, though, is a complicated terrain full of hazards and challenges that might compromise the fabric of real human connection.

The illusion of intimacy in online relationships is among their most obvious dangers. Social media channels show well chosen versions of our life, highlight reels highlighting the finest events while hiding the subtleties of our reality. This well chosen façade results in a distorted view of others that fuels comparison, inadequacy, and disconnection. Furthermore, the ease of online communication sometimes comes at the price of authenticity and depth since surface interactions and emoji-filled exchanges replace meaningful conversations.

The loss of privacy and boundaries is another danger of internet relationships. Personal data is sold for profit in the digital sphere, erasing the boundaries between public and private domains. Social media algorithms aggressively gather our information to customize ads and content. Furthermore, the never-ending stream of notifications and alerts can erode our sense of limits, causing an ongoing digital intrusion and overwhelm.

Social media channels also provide forums for online harassment, echo chambers, and false information. The anonymity the internet affords empowers people to act in ways they would never do in in-person interactions. Together with the viral character of online content, this anonymity can magnify the dissemination of false information and hate speech, so polarizing and dividing internet communities. Furthermore, the ubiquity of social media might aggravate loneliness and isolation since people evaluate their life against the well chosen highlight reels of others, which causes social exclusion and inadequacy.

In negotiating the dangers of internet relationships, one must develop awareness and judgment. Understand that social media is a two-edged sword—a tool capable of both connecting and separating, boosting and undercutting. Approach online interactions critically, challenging the validity and authenticity of the material you come across. Practice digital hygiene also by controlling your online use, organizing your digital surroundings, and protecting your security and privacy.

Utilizing Technology to Enhance, Not Replace, Real Relationships

Although social media and technology present many difficulties for real human connection, they also present chances for improving and strengthening real relationships. When used deliberately and with awareness, technology can be a great tool for enhancing relationships with others, communicating, and creating connection.

Technology's capacity to enable long-distance communication and cross geographic spaces is among its most important benefits. Regardless of physical distance, platforms including video calling, messaging apps, and social media help us to keep in touch with friends, relatives, and loved ones. These instruments let us share events, communicate ideas, and support each other over great distances, preserving relationships in a world growing more globalized.

Technology also provides a wealth of tools for improving common experiences and building deep bonds. Technology offers a wide range of chances for friendship and camaraderie from virtual events and online communities to group projects and common interests. These digital environments unite people with similar passions, interests, and values, fostering a feeling of connection and belonging.

Moreover, technology can act as a spur for personal development and self-expression inside couples. Social media channels let people express themselves authentically and interact with like-minded people by providing venues for sharing ideas, experiences, and artistic projects. Technology also offers access to support systems, self-help tools, and instructional materials that might improve our emotional health and strengthen our relationships.

Maintaining a balance between online and offline interactions is absolutely essential in using technology to improve actual relationships. In your online interactions, give quality more importance than quantity; concentrate on deep connections that strengthen your relationships and support your well-being.

Managing Digital Boundaries

Establishing and preserving digital boundaries that guard our well-being and promote positive relationships is crucial as we negotiate the challenging terrain of social media and technology. Digital boundaries refer to a spectrum of activities and habits that control our online presence, consumption, and interactions, ensuring that technology improves rather than compromises our quality of life.

Developing awareness of our online habits and behaviors is one of the first steps toward controlling digital boundaries. Examine your digital consumption patterns, including time spent online, platforms you visit, and how your online interactions affect your mental and emotional well-being. This self-awareness lays the groundwork for setting limits consistent with your priorities and values.

Clearly define your online behavior, impose limits on the time spent on social media, news reading, and digital entertainment. Set aside particular times to check social media and emails; fight the need to continuously update your feeds or answer alarms. In your daily schedule, also think about setting aside technology-free zones or times when you cut off screens and participate in offline activities meant to nourish your body, mind, and spirit.

Moreover, by establishing expectations and honest communication with others, develop good digital limits in your interactions. Talk to friends, relatives, and other loved ones about your choices and limits around digital communication, social media use, and privacy. Respect one another's preferences and limits and consider how your internet activity might affect others.

By routinely auditing your digital environment, curating your social media feeds, and unfollowing accounts that encourage toxicity or negativity, you practice digital hygiene. Use strong passwords, two-factor authentication, and awareness of the material you post on social media sites to help protect your privacy and security online.

Negotiating social media and technology calls for a sophisticated strategy that strikes a mix between the advantages and drawbacks of digital connectivity. Understanding the dangers of online interactions, using technology to improve real relationships, and controlling digital boundaries will help us to maximize technology and improve our life by means of genuine connections. By means of deliberate and conscious use of technology, we can foster relationships anchored in authenticity, respect, and real connection.

5 Things to Consider

Cultivate Digital Awareness: Think about your internet habits and behaviors, including social media time spent and how digital interactions affect your well-being. Think about how your online presence fits your priorities and values and be aware of the possible dangers of digital connection.

Balance Virtual and Physical Connections: Recognizing the value of both online and offline interactions, try to balance virtual and physical interactions. In your online interactions, give quality more importance than volume and concentrate on significant relationships that support real human connection and intimacy.

Practice Digital Hygiene: Set limits on internet use, curate your social media feeds, and protect your privacy and security online to help to keep a healthy digital surrounding. Review your digital habits and behaviors often; then, act to reduce digital overwhelm and intrusion.

Cultivate Mindful Technology Use: Approach technology use with mindfulness and intentionality, stressing how digital tools might improve rather than replace actual relationships. Use technology to enable deep connections, promote common experiences, and magnify voices that might otherwise be ignored.

Communicate Openly About Digital Boundaries: Talk candidly about digital limits and expectations with friends, relatives, and loved ones. Respect one another's choices and limits on internet use, and consider how your actions might affect others. Try to design digital spaces that encourage authenticity, connection, and respect.

Reflection Questions

How do my online habits and behaviors impact my overall well-being and quality of life? What steps can I take to cultivate greater awareness and mindfulness in my digital interactions?

In what ways do I prioritize virtual connections over physical ones, and vice versa? How can I strike a healthier balance between online and offline interactions to foster genuine human connection and intimacy?

What measures do I currently have in place to maintain a healthy digital environment and safeguard my privacy and security online?

How can I improve my digital hygiene practices to minimize digital overwhelm and intrusion?

How do I currently utilize technology to enhance, rather than replace, real relationships? Are there opportunities for me to leverage digital tools to foster meaningful connections, facilitate shared experiences, and amplify marginalized voices within my online communities?

How effectively do I communicate with others about digital boundaries and expectations? How can I engage in more open and honest conversations with friends, family, and loved ones about our shared digital experiences, preferences, and concerns?

Chapter 6
Investing in Mutual Growth

"We advise a man to regard his friends as highly as himself, to reflect that an enemy may become a friend, to stimulate love in the friend, and to check hatred in the enemy."
Seneca

Investing in mutual development is one of the most enriching and satisfying things one can do on the road of creating and preserving meaningful relationships. This chapter looks at the influence of helping one another toward goals and aspirations, of sharing values and beliefs, and of celebrating successes together. These components are the foundation of a dynamic and strong relationship in which the interaction of each person fosters and magnifies their personal development.

Supporting Each Other's Goals and Aspirations

One of the most important ways to show connection to both yourself and others is your dedication to personal development. The core of this dedication is the dynamic interaction between supporting each other's goals and aspirations, fostering both individual and group flourishing.

Supporting another's goals calls for a careful mix of sympathy, encouragement, and useful help. It starts with the skill of active listening—that is, really hearing and comprehending the dreams and aspirations of people we know. This kind of listening goes beyond simple respect; it entails interacting with their vision, appreciating the intellectual and emotional work supporting their goals. Verifying their objectives helps us to respect their value and possibilities, building a basis of mutual respect and trust.

Moreover, support shows in the readiness to provide direction and helpful criticism. This is about offering ideas that might help them be more refined and powerful than about imposing our own ideas or directions. It requires a sophisticated approach whereby feedback is given with compassion and encouragement is counterbalanced with honesty. By doing this, we enable a situation whereby aspirations can be pursued with confidence and clarity.

Another vital component is practical support. This can mean lending time and space for them to work on their projects, or distributing resources and networking chances. Our behavior shows our dedication to their development and supports the belief that their success is intertwined with our general welfare. This reciprocity promotes investment and a shared goal, strengthening the depth and resilience of the relationship.

From a more general standpoint, helping each other to achieve also means appreciating the socio-cultural settings that mold our ambitions. Knowing the external elements—such as social, cultural, or financial ones—that affect one's capacity to follow their objectives helps us to offer more specialized and significant assistance. It underlines the need of solidarity and empathy in negotiating the complexity of ambition and success.

Sharing Values and Beliefs

Any deep and committed relationship is built on shared values and beliefs. They provide a shared framework that directs our behavior, choices, and interactions, establishing coherence and alignment. Investing in mutual development by means of shared values and beliefs entails the respect of differences as well as the awareness of common ground.

Fundamentally, open, honest communication is what starts the sharing of values and beliefs. This calls for a readiness to express our own values precisely and pay attention to others' points of view free from judgment. By means of communication, we uncover the values guiding our behavior and choices, enabling us to coordinate our efforts for personal development.

Sharing values is mostly about being able to negotiate and traverse differences. Values and beliefs will inevitably vary in any relationship. These variations should be seen as chances for development and enrichment, not as challenges. Engaging many points of view helps us to widen our own knowledge and build a more inclusive and dynamic framework for personal development.

Furthermore, common values offer us a moral and ethical compass to direct our choices and interactions. They build responsibility and accountability, strengthening the integrity of the relationship. Operating from a place of shared values helps us to be coherent and purposeful, improving the depth and quality of our relationship.

Sharing values and beliefs also entails ongoing introspection and reassessment. Our values might change with time both personally and collectively. Maintaining an open communication and encouraging a culture of mutual respect and curiosity helps us to create a dynamic and always growing environment. This flexibility guarantees that our relationship stays vivid and sensitive to the evolving surroundings and difficulties we encounter.

Within the framework of mutual development, common values and beliefs serve both as a basis and a lighthouse. They give the stability required to negotiate uncertainty and the motivation to follow our goals with honesty and integrity.

Celebrating Successes Together

Celebrating achievements with others is a potent statement of solidarity and personal development. It strengthens the ties of relationship and promotes group happiness and accomplishment. This approach entails appreciating and celebrating every person in the relationship as well as the group successes resulting from group projects.

Celebrating starts with acknowledging—that is, spending time to value the accomplishments of others. This appreciation covers the little successes and advancement made along the way in addition to major ones. Celebrating these events helps us to respect the efforts and contributions of these people, boosting their motivation and self-worth.

Besides, celebration is a great inspiration and motivator. It starts a positive feedback loop whereby success is greeted with delight and encouragement, so motivating next projects and goals. In group projects, where shared successes magnify the feeling of group purpose and accomplishment, this dynamic is especially strong.

Celebrating with others also entails designing unforgettable events. Simple thanks and recognition to more complex ceremonies and events—these celebrations can take many different forms. The secret is to design surroundings in which people feel valued, seen, and appreciated. These happy times become treasured memories that enhance the emotional ties and resilience of the marriage.

From a more general standpoint, celebrating achievements together helps to foster a positive and supporting culture. It creates a setting where people are urged to pursue excellence, follow their dreams, and take chances. Maintaining both personally and group long-term development and well-being depends on this celebration and support culture.

Investing in mutual development, then, calls for a multifarious strategy covering helping each other's goals and aspirations, sharing values and beliefs, and celebrating successes together. We help the aspirations of people we love by means of active listening, constructive criticism, and useful support. When we clearly and ethically align our values, our actions and choices follow from one another. And we strengthen the ties of connection and create a positive and growing culture by means of the happy celebration of successes. Navigating these dynamics helps us to build resilient and transforming relationships in addition to deep and significant ones.

5 Things to Consider

Active Listening and Engagement: Truly listen to the goals and aspirations of those you care about. Engage with their vision by asking questions, offering encouragement, and showing genuine interest. This active involvement not only supports their ambitions but also strengthens your relationship by demonstrating that you value their dreams and efforts.

Balancing Encouragement and Constructive Feedback: While encouragement is essential, it's equally important to provide constructive feedback that can help refine and strengthen their goals. Approach feedback with empathy and compassion, ensuring that it is helpful and supportive rather than critical. Striking this balance fosters an environment where both parties can grow and improve.

Cultivating Shared Values and Beliefs: Reflect on the values and beliefs that underpin your actions and decisions. Engage in open dialogues to explore and understand the values of those close to you. Finding common ground while respecting differences can create a strong ethical and moral foundation for your relationship, guiding your collective actions and decisions.

Creating Meaningful Celebrations: Celebrate each other's successes in meaningful ways that resonate with both of you. This could range from simple acts of acknowledgment and gratitude to more elaborate rituals and gatherings. Celebrations should be personal and memorable, reinforcing the bonds of connection and creating cherished memories.

Recognizing and Addressing Socio-Cultural Contexts: Be aware of the socio-cultural contexts that influence your and your partner's goals and aspirations. Understanding these external factors can help you provide more tailored and meaningful support. Acknowledging and navigating these complexities together fosters empathy and solidarity, strengthening your mutual commitment to growth.

Reflection Questions

How well do I listen to and engage with the goals and aspirations of those I care about? In what ways can I improve my active listening skills to better support their dreams and ambitions?

How do I balance encouragement with constructive feedback when supporting others in their pursuits? Are there instances where I could have provided more helpful feedback or encouragement?

What values and beliefs are central to my life, and how do they align with those of my close relationships? How can we navigate and celebrate our shared values while respecting and learning from our differences?

How do I currently celebrate the successes of those close to me? Are there ways to make these celebrations more meaningful and personal to reinforce our connection and create lasting memories?

How aware am I of the socio-cultural contexts that shape the goals and aspirations of those around me? How can I better understand and address these external factors to provide more nuanced and empathetic support?

Chapter 7
Handling Conflict and Resolution

"Men are disturbed not by things, but by the views which they take of things."
Epictetus

Conflict is a normal part of relationships between people. There will always be times when two people don't agree or understand each other, no matter how close they are or how much they care about each other. The real test of a relationship is not how well it works when there is conflict, but how well it works when there is conflict with grace, empathy, and understanding.

This chapter talks about the art of conflict resolution and how to handle disagreements in a healthy way. It also talks about how to fix relationships that have been damaged and lets you know when it's time to let go. These things are necessary for keeping relationships healthy and strong, whether they're between friends, family, or romantic partners.

To deal with disagreements in a constructive way, you need to change the way you think. We need to stop seeing conflict as a failure or something we should try to avoid at all costs and start seeing it as a chance to grow and understand each other better. When handled carefully, conflict can show how a relationship works behind the scenes, bring up tensions that have been there for a while, and ultimately make connections stronger and more resilient.

Addressing Disagreements Constructively

Disagreements are inevitable in any relationship, whether it be between friends, family members, or romantic partners. When handled effectively, conflict can be an opportunity for growth, deeper understanding, and strengthening connections. However, when approached poorly, disagreements can lead to resentment, disconnection, and sometimes the dissolution of the relationship. Addressing disagreements constructively is thus a critical skill in fostering healthy, resilient relationships.

One of the first steps to addressing disagreements constructively is to recognize that conflict does not inherently signify a failure in the relationship. On the contrary, conflict is a natural part of human interaction. When two individuals with unique perspectives, values, and experiences come together, differences will arise. Rather than avoiding conflict or perceiving it as something to fear, we should instead view it as an opportunity to engage with and understand each other more deeply.

Constructive disagreement requires a commitment to respectful communication. The language we use during conflict can either escalate tensions or diffuse them. When emotions run high, it can be easy to resort to accusatory or confrontational language, but such reactions often make things worse. Instead, focus on "I" statements that express how you feel and what you need, rather than blaming the other person. For example, saying *"I feel hurt when..."* instead of *"You always..."* prevents the conversation from becoming adversarial and centers the discussion on emotions and needs, which are more vulnerable but also more productive.

Listening is just as important as speaking in these moments. Often during disagreements, people focus more on formulating their rebuttal rather than truly hearing the other person. This creates a cycle where neither party feels understood, and the disagreement deepens. To avoid this, practice active listening—really paying attention to what the other person is saying without interruption or judgment. Acknowledge their feelings and validate their perspective, even if you don't agree with it. Validating doesn't mean conceding; it means showing empathy and respect for their experience, which can diffuse defensiveness and open the door to compromise.

Timing also plays an essential role in addressing disagreements constructively. Not every moment is ideal for resolving conflict. When emotions are heated, and tensions are high, attempting to resolve the issue in the moment can lead to unproductive and hurtful exchanges. Instead, it might be wise to take a pause, allow emotions to cool down, and revisit the issue at a time when both parties can approach the conversation with a clearer mind. This kind of emotional regulation is crucial in keeping the conversation productive and focused on resolution rather than exacerbating the conflict.

The goal of addressing disagreements should not be to "win" but to find a resolution that honors both parties' needs. Approaching conflict with a mindset of collaboration rather than competition shifts the focus from right and wrong to finding common ground. This requires humility, openness, and a willingness to compromise. Recognize that the relationship is often more important than being right, and be willing to prioritize the connection over the argument.

Repairing Relationships After Conflict

Conflict can leave lasting damage if not properly addressed. Even when disagreements are handled constructively, the emotional aftermath can linger. Feelings of hurt, betrayal, or misunderstanding may persist, making it difficult for the relationship to return to its previous state. Repairing relationships after conflict is an essential process that requires intentional effort and vulnerability.

The first step in repairing a relationship after conflict is acknowledging the emotional impact of the disagreement. It's important to give space for any lingering emotions and to validate each other's feelings. This means recognizing the hurt that may have been caused, even if it was unintentional, and offering a sincere apology if necessary. Apologies should be genuine and not perfunctory; they should reflect an understanding of the impact of one's actions and a commitment to do better in the future. This helps rebuild trust and shows a willingness to be accountable for one's role in the conflict.

However, apologies alone are not enough to fully repair a relationship. Rebuilding trust requires consistent actions that demonstrate a commitment to positive change. For instance, if the conflict arose from repeated behavior that one party found hurtful, the offending party must make an effort to address that behavior moving forward. Repairing relationships after conflict means not just promising change but actively working towards it.

In some cases, outside help may be beneficial. Some conflicts are deeply rooted in misunderstandings or differences that individuals struggle to resolve on their own. Seeking the guidance of a mediator, therapist, or counselor can provide new perspectives and tools for navigating the situation. This kind of intervention can offer a neutral space where both parties feel heard and supported in finding a resolution.

Reconciliation also requires patience. Depending on the severity of the conflict, it may take time for wounds to heal. It's important to allow for this process without rushing it. Forcing resolution prematurely can lead to unresolved issues festering beneath the surface, potentially causing further conflict down the line. Patience allows for genuine healing and ensures that when the relationship is repaired, it is built on a stronger, more resilient foundation.

Repairing a relationship after conflict is not only about addressing the immediate issue but also about reflecting on what the conflict reveals about the broader dynamics within the relationship. Use the conflict as an opportunity to examine patterns of behavior, communication styles, and underlying tensions that may need attention. By addressing these larger issues, you can prevent similar conflicts from arising in the future and create a healthier, more harmonious connection moving forward.

Knowing When to Let Go

Not every relationship can or should be saved after conflict. Sometimes, the healthiest and most compassionate choice is to let go. This can be one of the most difficult decisions to make, especially in close relationships where emotional investment runs deep. However, knowing when to let go is a vital part of maintaining personal well-being and integrity.

Letting go often begins with recognizing when a relationship is no longer serving the well-being of either party. If repeated conflicts arise without resolution, if one party consistently disrespects the boundaries of the other, or if the relationship becomes emotionally or physically harmful, it may be time to consider ending the connection. Relationships should be a source of support, respect, and mutual growth. When these elements are persistently absent, the relationship may be doing more harm than good.

Letting go does not necessarily mean giving up. It can be a conscious choice to prioritize one's emotional and mental health over maintaining a connection that is damaging. It's important to recognize that while conflict is a natural part of relationships, constant or unresolved conflict can create a toxic environment. Choosing to remove oneself from such an environment is an act of self-care and self-preservation.

Knowing when to let go also involves accepting that not all relationships are meant to last forever. People grow, change, and sometimes outgrow their connections. Letting go can be a natural part of the life cycle of relationships, rather than a failure. It's an acknowledgment that while the relationship may have been meaningful at one point, it no longer aligns with who you are or what you need.

The process of letting go requires grieving. Even in cases where the relationship has become toxic or damaging, there is often a sense of loss that accompanies the decision to end it. Allowing space for grief is essential in the healing process. It's important to honor the emotional attachment that existed and to give oneself permission to feel the sadness, anger, or relief that may come with the decision.

Letting go opens the door for new possibilities. It creates space for new relationships to emerge, ones that are healthier, more supportive, and more aligned with your values and needs. Letting go is not the end of connection but the beginning of a new chapter, one where personal well-being and mutual respect take precedence over unresolved conflict and tension.

5 Things to Consider

Conflict Is an Opportunity for Growth: Instead of avoiding conflict, recognize it as a chance to deepen understanding and strengthen relationships. When handled constructively, disagreements can reveal underlying issues and lead to positive change.

Communication Is Key: The way you communicate during conflict can either escalate or de-escalate the situation. Focus on using respectful, non-accusatory language, and practice active listening to better understand the other person's perspective.

Repair Takes Time and Effort: Healing after conflict requires patience and intentionality. Apologies are important, but actions that show a commitment to change and growth are equally necessary to rebuild trust and strengthen the bond.

Not All Conflicts Can Be Resolved: Some relationships may reach a point where conflict is a sign of deeper incompatibility or harm. It's important to recognize when a relationship is no longer serving your well-being and when it's healthier to let go.

Emotional Regulation Matters: Managing your emotions during conflict is crucial. Taking time to cool down and process emotions before addressing an issue can lead to more constructive and productive conversations, preventing unnecessary escalation.

Reflection Questions

How do I typically respond to conflict in my relationships, and what impact does this have on the outcome of disagreements?

In what ways can I improve my communication during disagreements to ensure that I am both expressing my needs clearly and listening to the other person with empathy and respect?

When conflict arises, am I able to recognize when a situation needs time and space to cool down, or do I tend to push for immediate resolution? How can I better manage my emotions during these moments?

What steps have I taken in the past to repair relationships after conflict, and were these efforts effective in rebuilding trust and understanding? What could I do differently in the future?

How do I know when it's time to let go of a relationship that is no longer healthy or beneficial? What signs should I pay attention to in recognizing when conflict has become too damaging to resolve?

Chapter 8

Balancing Social Life with Personal Time

"The mind must be given relaxation, it will rise improved and sharper after a good break. Just as rich fields must not be forced... so constant work on the anvil will fracture the force of the mind."

Seneca

Finding a balance between social life and personal time is harder than ever in a world that is becoming more and more connected. The constant pull of technology, social events, and the need to stay in touch can make it hard to find time to be alone and think. Still, finding a balance between time spent with others and time spent alone is important for mental health, emotional well-being, and overall health.

In this chapter, the tricky art of balancing social interactions with personal time is looked at. The need for solitude, self-care, and smart energy management in social situations are emphasized. It talks about how important it is to put yourself first while still having meaningful relationships with other people. It also talks about how important it is to know your own limits, preferences, and boundaries when it comes to socializing.

Instead of seeing being alone and being social as opposites, this chapter looks at them as parts of a fulfilling life that work together.

Both are important to our health and happiness. Social connections make our lives better through shared experiences and relationships, while solitude gives us a chance to think, be creative, and grow as people.

To find balance between these two sides, you need to know yourself, be able to set limits, and keep your energy in check. To help you find that balance, this chapter will give you ideas on how to keep your deep and meaningful relationships without losing yourself. The goal is to create a life where you can balance alone time with social interactions in a way that benefits both you and the people you connect with.

Making Self-Care a Priority

Self-care is important for keeping a healthy balance between social life and personal well-being in a time that values always being connected and involved. Self-care is the act of taking care of your own physical, mental, and emotional health on purpose. It's about realizing that social interactions can be helpful, but they can also be draining if they get in the way of your own needs. To have a meaningful social life, you need to take care of your own needs.

Being socially active all the time can be too much for some people, and they forget to take care of themselves. Society often praises the idea of always being available, whether it's through social media, group activities, or networking at work. This makes it hard to be alone or think about oneself. This never-ending engagement often leads to exhaustion, burnout, and a feeling of being cut off from oneself.

Self-care is very personal and can include simple things like reading a book, going for a walk, or meditating, as well as more structured things like therapy or setting aside time for "me time." Self-care, in any form, is meant to give you a sense of renewal and help you find your center in a world that is always calling for your attention. This focus on the self helps restore energy and emotional clarity, which are both necessary for having meaningful interactions with other people.

Also, putting yourself first doesn't mean giving up all social activities. Instead, it's about finding a balance where treating yourself well is just as important as spending time with other people. One important part of this practice is learning to say "no" to social events and time demands. It lets you set limits that are good for your health and help you be more present when you do choose to interact with other people.

Taking care of yourself every day gives you a sense of independence and control over your life. Knowing your limits and knowing when to step back are important parts of being mindful. Self-care is strange because it demands time from you, but it also lets you give more to other people and communities. This is because taking care of yourself lets you interact with others from a place of being whole and refilled, not worn out. Without this balance, relationships can become stressful instead of connecting, because being emotionally tired can make it harder to understand and care about other people.

Self-care is also a way to show respect for yourself. It tells yourself and other people that your health is important. Individuals around you may be inspired to value their own needs in social situations by the way you act in this situation. By putting yourself first, you build a base for all of your interactions, whether they are personal, professional, or social.

Finding a Balance Between Being Alone and Being with Other People

It's hard to find a good balance between being social and being alone, especially in a culture that often associates being outgoing with success. To be emotionally and mentally healthy in the long term, you need to be able to keep this balance. Being alone and spending time with other people are not opposites; they are both important for living a full life. Each one helps with mental health, personal growth, and creativity in its own way.

Socializing lets you get to know other people, share your experiences, and feel like you belong. People are naturally social, and interacting with others is important for our mental health. Having meaningful interactions with other people can make our lives better by giving us support, stimulation, and joy. Being close to family, friends, and even strangers on a regular basis shapes who we are and helps us figure out how to get around in the world.

On the other hand, being alone is just as important. Being alone lets you think, be creative, and learn more about yourself. It gives you a place to work through your feelings, think about your experiences, and learn more about yourself. Spending time by yourself can help you see things that are easier to see when you're not with other people. For many, being alone is a safe place where they can recharge and feel calm again.

Mindful self-awareness is needed to find a balance between being alone and being with other people. To start, you need to be aware of your own wants and needs. Some people may do best in places with lots of other people, getting energy and ideas from being around other people all the time. Others may feel worn out from too much socializing and need regular times alone to keep their emotions in check. The first thing you need to do to find a balance that works for you is to understand your own habits.

It is important to get rid of the idea that people are naturally either "social" or "solitary." Most people are somewhere in the middle, and their needs may change depending on their emotions, stress levels, and the situation they are in. Realizing that these needs change over time lets you find a better balance between being alone and being with other people. There will be times in your life when you want to connect with others more than others, and times when you'd rather be alone.

A big part of finding this balance is setting limits. It's important to know when to say "no" to social invitations, take time for yourself, and get back to talking to people. It's not about sticking to a strict schedule; it's about being aware of your emotional and mental needs and meeting them. To find a balance between social life and alone time, you need to be aware of your inner state and talk to yourself about what you need right now.

The balance between being alone and being with other people changes over time. As things in your life change, you have to keep adjusting and fine-tuning it. How you find this balance will depend on things like work, family duties, and personal stressors. You can keep meaningful social connections without giving up your sense of self if you are flexible and aware of your own needs.

Keeping Track of Energy and Social Activities

One of the most overlooked parts of having a balanced social life is managing your energy when it comes to social events. Getting involved with other people takes energy, and depending on the type of interaction, it can either give you energy or drain it. To stay in balance, you need to know how to control your energy and know what kinds of interactions give you energy and what kinds drain it.

Every time two people talk to each other, they exchange energy. You feel more alive and inspired when you're with certain people or in certain situations. These are the connections that make you feel better, more supported, and lifted. Having said that, some social activities can be draining and leave you feeling emotionally worn out. It's possible that this is because of how the relationship works or because of the demands of the situation.

Figuring out which social situations give you energy and which ones drain you is the first thing you need to do to manage your energy. This requires you to think about and pay attention to how you feel before, during, and after social events. Pay attention to how you feel after being in certain places or with certain people. Are you feeling energized and happy, or are you tired and stressed? You can start to make decisions that put your health first once you see the patterns.

It is important to know that you can only have so much energy. In the same way that physical energy drops after working out, emotional and social energy can drop after long or intense social events. This is why it's important to plan time to relax after social events that are especially demanding. Giving yourself time to rest and recharge will make sure you have the energy to interact fully with others when you decide to.

Knowing your social bandwidth is another important part of managing your energy. When you talk about social bandwidth, you mean how much social interaction you can handle at once without getting too busy. Different things, like stress, work, personal problems, and even the time of year, can change your bandwidth. Knowing your social bandwidth will help you avoid taking on too many social activities that will drain you.

Managing your energy means being picky about how and with whom you spend your time. Relationships that bring you happiness, support, and good vibes should be your top priority. This doesn't mean you should stay away from all tough or emotionally taxing situations, but you should be aware of the balance between giving and receiving energy in your relationships.

Lastly, being in tune with the rhythms of your own life is another part of managing your energy. Your energy level will go up and down. Sometimes you'll feel like spending time with other people, and other times you'll need to take a break and focus on yourself. Being aware of these cycles and adjusting your social obligations accordingly can help you stay in balance without getting too busy or worn out.

Finding a good balance between social life and personal time requires smart energy management, deliberate self-care, and a deep understanding of how being alone and with others affect each other. If you get these things to work together, they make a stable foundation for a healthy, fulfilling social life that doesn't hurt your own health.

5 Things to Consider

Self-Care is Essential: Prioritizing self-care is not selfish; it's a necessary practice for maintaining your mental, emotional, and physical well-being. Without taking care of yourself, social interactions can quickly become draining rather than fulfilling.

Balance Socializing and Solitude: Both socializing and solitude serve essential roles in a fulfilling life. Social interactions provide connection and support, while solitude offers space for self-reflection and personal growth. Striking a balance between the two is key to long-term well-being.

Understand Your Energy Levels: Social interactions require energy, and not all engagements have the same impact. Pay attention to how different social situations affect you, and prioritize relationships and activities that energize rather than drain you.

Set Clear Boundaries: Setting and communicating boundaries helps you protect your personal time and emotional well-being. Saying no to social engagements when you need personal time is crucial to maintaining balance and avoiding burnout.

Recognize Social Bandwidth: Your capacity for social engagement can fluctuate depending on stress levels, personal challenges, or life circumstances. Being mindful of your social bandwidth allows you to make more intentional choices about when to engage with others and when to prioritize solitude.

Reflection Questions

How do I currently prioritize self-care in my daily life, and what changes could I make to ensure that my personal needs are met alongside my social commitments?

What signals do I notice in myself when I've had too much social interaction or too little solitude, and how can I respond more effectively to maintain balance?

Which social activities or relationships energize me, and which ones tend to leave me feeling drained? How can I adjust my social engagements to prioritize those that uplift me?

Am I setting and communicating clear boundaries between my social life and personal time? How can I improve at saying "no" when I need to protect my personal space?

What strategies can I implement to better manage my social bandwidth and avoid overcommitting to activities that may overwhelm me emotionally or mentally?

Chapter 9
Exploring Activities That Strengthen Bonds

"There is no possession more valuable than a good and faithful friend."
Socrates

You can't say enough about how hobbies and interests that people share can bring us closer together. People who are involved in activities that other people or groups enjoy feel more connected to each other than just socially. These shared experiences help people grow closer to each other by building relationships based on understanding, fun, and working together.

Hobbyists don't just do things for fun; they show who they are, what they love, and how creative they are. Some people share parts of themselves when they do activities they enjoy together. Sharing with each other builds a base of commonality where differences are emphasized and similarities are emphasized. For example, two people who both love painting might become close over different painting styles, color schemes, or artists they both like. When they talk about and do things related to this hobby, they share a common language and set of experiences that make their relationship stronger.

Groups often form a sense of shared identity when people share interests. When a group of friends gets together often to do things like play music, go hiking, or cook, they stop seeing themselves as individuals and start seeing themselves as part of a cohesive unit. A sense of belonging is important for the emotional and mental health of the people in the group, and this shared identity helps build that. People in the group find support, motivation, and inspiration in each other, which makes the bonds between them stronger.

Hobbies that people share also help people work together and collaborate. When people join a book club, a team sport, or a group art project, they have to work together to reach a common goal. Working together on this project builds trust and reinforces the idea that everyone's contribution is important. This trust builds into stronger emotional bonds and a stronger sense of community over time.

Also, hobbies that bring people together can help them connect when they might not be able to otherwise. A common interest can help people in a group who come from different cultures, backgrounds, or life experiences get along with each other. It turns into a place where differences are not only accepted, but also praised for making the experience more meaningful for everyone. This openness makes the bonds between people in the group stronger, making society more able to handle the problems that come up because of diversity.

It's important to remember that hobbies have benefits beyond just making people friends. Doing things that make you happy and fulfilled can lower stress, improve your mental health, and make you happier with your life in general. The good effects are amplified when these activities are done with other people, because socializing itself is good for your health. This starts a positive cycle where strong bonds make people want to do fun things together more often, which makes the bonds even stronger.

Technology, work, and the demands of daily life can make people feel alone, but hobbies bring people together in a way that is very helpful. They make it possible for people to get together, be present, and interact with each other in deep ways. These things help us remember how much joy there is in simple, shared experiences and how they can change our relationships in big ways.

Trips and Activities for Groups

Group trips and experiences are great ways to get to know each other better because they create memories that become part of the group's history. Whether it's a camping trip over the weekend, a road trip, or a difficult hike, these kinds of adventures bring people together in ways that are hard to find in everyday life.

One reason why group adventures are so good for building relationships is that they often require people to leave their comfort zone. People face new problems and unknowns when they go on an adventure together. People can become closer when they know they can count on each other for support and encouragement. The sense of accomplishment that comes from overcoming these problems as a group strengthens the bonds between its members, fostering a strong sense of friendship.

A break from everyday life is another thing that adventures do. They help people see each other in a new way. People often show sides of themselves that they might not show in more normal situations when they are on an adventure. On a group hike, someone who is usually quiet might step up and lead, and on a road trip, someone who is usually serious might show their playful side. The relationship is stronger now that they know more about each other's personalities.

The memories that everyone in the group makes on group adventures also serve as a point of reference for the group. These events become stories that are told and relived, which makes the connection stronger each time they are brought up. The adventure becomes a part of the group's identity and a moment that brings them all together. For example, when a group of friends travels together, they may have inside jokes, rituals, or a shared understanding that makes their bond stronger.

Going on adventures with a group is also a great way to build trust. When people are in places or situations they don't know well, they need to depend on each other more than they normally would. This dependence builds trust because people in the group show that they can be counted on and are committed to each other. Trust is an important part of any good relationship, and going on adventures with a group is a natural way to build it.

Along with trust, group adventures usually require a lot of working together as a team. Members of a group must work together to reach their objectives, whether they are setting up a campsite, getting around a new city, or making plans for a trip. Working together builds a sense of unity and a common goal, which makes the bonds between members stronger.

Group adventures are often a way to escape the stresses and routines of everyday life. This break can be very relaxing and give you a new perspective. It can also help you feel closer to the people you spent time with during the experience. The freedom and exploration that come with going on a group adventure can bring back the spark in relationships and make them feel more alive and full of life.

Going on adventures and experiences with a group is a great way to strengthen relationships because it lets people be vulnerable, builds trust, and makes memories that will last a lifetime. These trips remind us how much fun it is to discover new things and how important it is to get out of our comfort zones in order to connect with others in meaningful ways.

Making Customs and Traditions

Traditions and rituals are important for making and keeping strong bonds with other people. People in a group feel like they belong and have an identity when they do these things over and over again. Whether they are as simple as a weekly dinner or as big as a holiday party every year, traditions and rituals help people connect and share experiences on a regular basis.

One big reason why traditions and rituals are so good at strengthening bonds is that they make people feel safe and sure of what will happen. Traditions give people a safe and predictable way to live in a world that is often unpredictable and crazy. The members of the group feel safe because they know they can count on these rituals to bring them together on a regular basis. Over time, this predictability makes the emotional bonds between people in the group stronger.

Traditions are also a way for a group to honor its history and values. They help the group remember and celebrate what's important to them, like family, friends, or a belief they all share. For instance, when a family gets together every year for a holiday meal, they're not just sharing food; they're also reaffirming their love for each other and the things that are important to them. This reaffirmation makes the group's identity stronger and strengthens the bonds between its members.

Traditions and rituals also help people feel like they belong. When someone takes part in a tradition, they are doing something that is important to the group. People who take part feel like they are part of something bigger than themselves, which makes them feel like they belong and are included. This feeling of belonging is important for emotional health because it gives people a base of support and connection they can count on.

A strong symbolic function is served by rituals in particular. Symbols, actions, or words that have a deeper meaning for the group are often used in them. For example, friends who raise a glass to each other's health at the start of every get-together are doing more than just drinking together; they are also making a promise to look out for each other's health. These rituals give everyone a sense of a common meaning and purpose, which makes the bond between them stronger.

Rituals not only serve as symbols, but they also give people a chance to think and be mindful. Rituals often require people to slow down, be present, and pay attention to the present moment. Being aware of the present moment helps people feel more connected to the ritual and to each other. Slowly but surely, these mindful moments help the group grow closer and stronger.

Making new traditions and rituals is another great way to bring people closer together. When a group of people get together to start a new tradition, they are an active part of making their shared identity. This way of making the tradition gives people a sense of ownership and pride in it, which gives it more meaning for the group. People who decide to go camping once a year with their friends aren't just planning an event; they're making a tradition that will become a part of their history and identity.

Traditions and rituals are a way to mark and celebrate time. They give the group a way to remember important events, anniversaries, and changes in its life. Rituals like birthday parties, graduation parties, and retirement ceremonies give people a chance to think about the past, enjoy the present, and look forward to the future. This reflection makes the connection between group members stronger by reminding them of how important their shared journey is and how long the group has been together.

Traditions and rituals are important for making bonds stronger within a group. They give you a sense of security, belonging, and identity, and they also give you time to think and be mindful. Whether they are new traditions or old ones that have been around for a long time, these rituals are very important for making deep connections that last.

5 Things to Consider

Shared Interests Foster Deeper Connections: Engaging in hobbies and activities that you and others genuinely enjoy can create a strong foundation for deeper relationships. These shared experiences allow you to connect on a more personal level, making it easier to build trust and understanding.

Group Adventures Build Camaraderie: Participating in group adventures, such as trips or challenging activities, can strengthen bonds through shared challenges and memorable experiences. These adventures help build trust, encourage teamwork, and create lasting memories that reinforce the group's connection.

Traditions and Rituals Provide Stability: Establishing regular traditions or rituals within a group or relationship can create a sense of continuity and belonging. These recurring practices help reinforce shared values, provide emotional security, and strengthen the sense of identity within the group.

Vulnerability Enhances Bonding: Engaging in activities that require stepping outside of your comfort zone with others can create opportunities for vulnerability, which in turn fosters deeper emotional connections. These moments of shared vulnerability can be powerful in strengthening bonds.

The Symbolic Power of Rituals: Rituals, whether simple or elaborate, carry symbolic meaning that reinforces the values and identity of the group. Participating in these rituals mindfully can deepen the emotional connection between members and create a shared sense of purpose.

Reflection Questions

What hobbies or interests do I share with those close to me, and how can I invest more time in these activities to strengthen our connections?

How do I feel after participating in group adventures or shared experiences, and what specific activities have brought me closer to others in the past?

What traditions or rituals do I currently practice with friends, family, or groups, and how do these practices contribute to our sense of belonging and continuity?

In what ways have I stepped outside of my comfort zone with others, and how did these moments of vulnerability impact my relationships?

How can I be more mindful and intentional in participating in or creating rituals that reinforce the values and identity of my social circles?

Chapter 10

Nurturing Long-Distance Friendships

"For what purpose, then, do I make a man my friend? In order to have someone for whom I may die, whom I may follow into exile, against whose death I may stake my own life, and pay the pledge, too."
Seneca

One of the hardest things about long-distance friendships is keeping in touch. In a world where being close by often determines how strong relationships are, being far away can be a big problem. The core of a strong friendship doesn't change when people live far apart, though. It changes and adapts. To keep the bonds of friendship strong and even grow stronger over time, it's important to know how to care for these connections.

First, it's important to understand how long-distance friendships affect us emotionally. Being physically apart can make you feel lonely and disconnected, which can weaken the bond if you don't do anything about it. To fight this, it's important to keep in touch on a regular basis. Being consistent is very important; it helps to set up a rhythm that mirrors how you would naturally interact if you lived closer. This could mean setting aside times during the day to talk on the phone, video chat, or text. Making sure that the connection feels natural instead of forced, both people should be able to choose how often and how they want to talk to each other.

Staying connected with someone far away requires a level of emotional openness and vulnerability that might not be as important in relationships with people who live close by. If you don't have the ability to read body language or share spontaneous moments, talking to each other is the only way to express your feelings and stay close. This means that you should share your life, thoughts, and feelings more on purpose. It means going out of your way to show that person that they are still important in your life, even though you are far away.

Another important thing is that everyone needs to understand and be patient with each other. Friendships that last a long time usually need more work and flexibility. There will be times when one person is busier or less responsive than usual. It's important to deal with these times with understanding instead of anger. Being aware that life isn't always the same and that distance makes things more complicated can help you keep a healthy and strong connection. Also, it's important to keep your expectations in check. Although you might not be able to talk to your friend as much as you would with someone who lives close by, the connection can still be just as strong, if not stronger, if you take the right steps.

Sharing experiences, even if they're far away, is a key part of staying connected. This could mean watching the same movie or TV show and talking about it afterward, playing games online together, or doing something you both like online. By doing these things together, you make new memories and strengthen your relationship, which makes the distance feel less important.

Lastly, trust and commitment are important for keeping friendships alive over long distances. It's important to believe that the other person values the friendship as much as you do and to work hard to keep it going. Trust helps close the emotional gap that distance can make, and commitment makes sure that both people stay invested in the relationship even when things get tough.

Staying connected with someone far away requires planning, being emotionally open, understanding, shared experiences, and a strong base of trust and commitment. Even though being far away can be hard, it can also help you grow closer in ways that you might not have been able to before.

Using Technology to Keep in Touch with People Far Away

In this day and age of digital connections, technology is an important part of keeping in touch with friends who live far away. But the way we use technology can have a big effect on how well these relationships work. It's not enough to just stay in touch; you can use technology to add to the emotional depth and closeness that make friendships special, not take them away.

Communication platforms are one of the most obvious ways that technology helps friends who live far away stay in touch. Video calls, instant messaging, and social media make it easy for friends who live far away to stay in touch. People can share their daily thoughts, feelings, and experiences on these platforms, which helps to keep a sense of closeness. But you should be careful when you use these tools. Messages and texts are convenient, but because there are no body language, they can sometimes lead to misunderstandings. Video calls, on the other hand, are a more complete way to talk, letting you have deeper, more emotional conversations. Depending on the situation and what you need, using a mix of these technologies can help you keep your relationship healthy and happy.

Technology not only lets us talk to each other, but it also lets us do things together. Even if people are far away, they can feel like they are part of the same experience when they play games, read books, or work together on creative projects online. These things not only keep you entertained, but they also help you make new memories and keep the connection strong. For example, working together to play an online game can strengthen the bond between two people in a way similar to how doing a physical activity together can.

When used wisely, social media can also help people stay friends even though they live far away. Friends can stay up to date on each other's lives by sharing status updates, photos, and important events on social media sites like Facebook and Instagram. On the other hand, it's important to remember that social media often shows a skewed view of reality. So, it's important to keep the relationship real by talking to each other in a more personal and direct way in addition to social media.

Technology also makes it possible to send more physical signs of friendship, like letters, gifts, and care packages through online services. Even though these actions are made easier by technology, they still have a personal touch that can have a big effect on the emotional connection. A handwritten letter or thoughtfully chosen gift in the mail can feel more meaningful than a text message. It can help you feel like your friendship is valued and cared for.

But there are risks that can come up if you rely too much on technology to keep up long-distance relationships. One of these risks is giving in to the urge to value quantity over quality. It's simple to think that frequently having brief, surface-level conversations is enough to keep a friendship alive. To really stay connected, it's much more important to have deep conversations and share experiences, even if they don't happen as often.

Another danger is that people might get tired of using technology. Many times, being connected all the time can make interactions feel like work instead of fun, which is called burnout. It's important to know when this is happening and set limits that keep the relationship fun and spontaneous. Talking to each other at set times or being honest about when you need a break from technology could be part of this.

Technology can help you keep in touch with friends and family who live far away, but you have to be careful and deliberate about how you use it. Friends can use technology to stay close even when they live far apart by using a variety of ways to talk to each other, doing things together, and being aware of the risks that could come up.

Making Plans for Meaningful Visits

Even though technology is a big part of keeping up with friends who live far away, there is nothing like seeing them in person. Planning meaningful visits is an important part of keeping these relationships alive because they give you a chance to connect more deeply and make memories that will last a lifetime. But these visits need to be carefully planned and thought out to make sure they strengthen the friendship instead of putting it under stress.

Setting clear goals and expectations is the first thing that needs to be done to plan a meaningful visit. Both people should talk about what they want to get out of the visit, whether it's just hanging out and catching up on each other's lives, trying new things together, or just having fun. Knowing what the other person wants from the visit helps to make sure that it fits with the friendship's goals, leaving both people feeling happy and connected.

Another important factor is timing. Since these visits don't happen very often, it's important to pick a time that works for everyone, taking into account work schedules, personal obligations, and anything else that could affect the quality of the visit. Also, it's important to find a balance between making plans and just going with the flow. To get the most out of the time you have together, you need some structure, but letting things happen on the spot can add a fun and unexpected element to the visit.

Things that are planned to do during the visit should be related to the friends' shared interests and values. The goal should be to deepen the connection and create new shared experiences, whether it's going back to old favorites, seeing new places, or just spending time with each other. Don't try to cram too many things into a short amount of time or make too many plans. Over-the-top plans aren't what really strengthens the bond; quality time together is.

Also, these visits give you a chance to talk about any problems or worries that came up while you were apart. When you talk to someone in person, you can connect with them on an emotional level that is hard to do online. If there have been misunderstandings, bad communication, or unresolved problems, talking to each other in person during the visit can help clear the air and build trust and understanding in the friendship.

Space and boundaries are another important thing to think about when planning meaningful visits. You may want to spend all of your time together because you're so excited about the visit, but it's important to give each other space. This is especially true if you stay at each other's houses during the visit. Making sure that everyone feels safe and respected in their own space can help keep problems from happening and make the visit better overall.

Last but not least, it's important to have a thankful attitude before the visit. We shouldn't forget the work and resources that are needed to make these visits possible. Recognizing how important the visit was, being thankful for the time spent together, and cherishing the memories made can strengthen the bond and make both people feel valued and appreciated.

Planning meaningful visits is an important part of keeping long-distance friendships alive. Friends can get the most out of their time together and strengthen the emotional bond that keeps them friends across miles by being clear about their goals, picking the right time, focusing on quality over quantity, talking about any problems, giving each other space, and being thankful for the visit.

5 Things to Consider

Intentional Communication is Key: Maintaining a strong connection across distance requires regular, intentional communication. It's important to set aside time for meaningful conversations that go beyond surface-level interactions, ensuring that both parties feel connected and valued.

Leverage Technology Wisely: While technology offers numerous tools to stay in touch, it's crucial to use these tools mindfully. Balancing text messages, video calls, and social media interactions can help maintain a healthy and fulfilling long-distance friendship, but be cautious of digital fatigue and superficial interactions.

Plan Visits with Care: When planning in-person visits, focus on quality time and shared experiences that deepen the bond. Be mindful of each other's expectations, personal space, and the balance between planned activities and spontaneity to ensure a meaningful and enjoyable visit.

Trust and Patience are Essential: Long-distance friendships require a strong foundation of trust and patience. Understanding that life circumstances may sometimes limit communication or visits is important in maintaining a resilient and healthy relationship.

Shared Experiences Matter: Engaging in shared activities, even from a distance, can reinforce the connection and create new memories. Whether it's watching a movie together online, playing a game, or collaborating on a project, these shared moments help bridge the physical gap.

Reflection Questions

How do I currently communicate with my long-distance friends, and what steps can I take to ensure our interactions are meaningful and consistent?

In what ways am I using technology to maintain my long-distance friendships, and how can I improve my use of these tools to enhance our connection rather than just maintaining it?

When planning visits with long-distance friends, how do I balance the desire for shared experiences with the need for personal space and downtime?

How do I handle feelings of disconnection or loneliness in my long-distance friendships, and what strategies can I adopt to address these challenges constructively?

What shared activities or experiences have brought me closer to my long-distance friends, and how can I incorporate more of these into our relationship?

Chapter 11

The Role of Family in Your Social Circle

"To the gods I am indebted for having good grandfathers, good parents, a good sister, good teachers, good associates, good kinsmen and friends, nearly everything good."

Marcus Aurelius

Family relationships are important to most people because they give them support, love, and a sense of who they are. But because family is so important, it can be hard to balance family relationships with other kinds of relationships, like friendships, romantic partnerships, and professional groups. Figuring out how to handle these situations is important for keeping a positive and enjoyable social life.

To keep family and other relationships in balance, you need to know what role each type of relationship plays in your life. Family ties are often very strong and last a long time. These ties are usually based on shared history and cultural values. People in these kinds of relationships often feel a strong sense of duty and obligation that isn't as strong in other types of relationships. People may put family relationships ahead of other relationships, even if it means sacrificing personal growth or the growth of other important relationships.

To find balance, you need to understand that different relationships meet different needs. Having family relationships can give you a sense of continuity and belonging, while dating and friendships can give you new experiences, shared interests, and emotional support that you can't get from your family. Professional relationships, on the other hand, can be good for your mind, your career, and your ability to work together. To find the right balance between these different factors, you need to take a thoughtful approach that values the unique contributions of each relationship while making sure that none of them are ignored or given too much attention.

Managing time and energy is hard when you have family ties and other connections at the same time. Family duties can be hard to balance, leaving little time for other relationships. You should be there for family events, care for elderly relatives, or help your siblings. This is especially true in cultures or family structures where these things are expected. Even though these responsibilities are important, you also need to make time for other relationships that are good for your health and help you grow as a person.

You should also think about how family expectations affect your other relationships. When you choose who to spend time with, whether it's friends, romantic partners, or coworkers, your family may have strong feelings about it. Sometimes, these opinions can make things difficult, especially if they go against the things you've chosen or the way your other relationships work. To get through these situations, you need to be able to communicate clearly and know what your own values and priorities are. It's important to pay attention to what your family is worried about while also being firm about who you let into your social circle.

In some cases, balancing family relationships with other relationships may mean rethinking how intense and what kind of relationships you have with your family. Set limits on your family relationships if they are too demanding or emotionally draining. This will help you keep your time and energy for other relationships. This doesn't mean leaving your family behind; it means finding a good balance that lets you do well in all parts of your social life.

Also, it's important to be aware that family and other social connections can sometimes overlap. For example, bringing friends or romantic partners into the family can help everyone get along and support each other. However, it's important to carefully handle these overlaps to avoid any problems or misunderstandings. Being honest and talking to each other openly are important for making sure that everyone feels respected and valued.

Balancing family relationships with other relationships is a tricky job that needs awareness, planning, and clear communication. You can keep a healthy social circle that helps your personal growth and well-being by understanding the unique role each relationship plays in your life, managing your time and energy well, and setting healthy boundaries.

Setting Healthy Limits with Family Members

A key part of keeping a balanced and satisfying social life is setting healthy limits with family members. Family relationships can be very helpful emotionally and give you a sense of who you are, but they can also be tense and conflictual if limits are not set and followed. Setting healthy limits for yourself and your family helps you stay mentally and emotionally healthy and lets you interact with them in a way that is helpful and not too much.

Because of the strong emotional ties and high expectations that come with family relationships, setting boundaries can be harder than in other types of relationships. People learn early on what their role is in the family, whether it's as a caregiver, a mediator, or the "responsible one." These roles can become deeply ingrained and hard to change, which can cause people to interact in ways that aren't always healthy or good for personal growth.

Finding out where your needs or limits are not being respected is the first thing you need to do to set healthy boundaries with family members. This could mean being aware of when family duties are taking up too much of your time, when a family member's behavior is making you feel emotionally drained, or when you feel like you have to conform to family expectations that go against your own values or goals. Once you know what these areas are, it's important to be clear and firm about your boundaries.

Setting limits with family members can be hard, especially if there is a history of fighting or if the family culture doesn't allow for open conversations about personal needs. However, it's important to be honest and caring when having these talks. You should be polite and not blame others when you talk about your needs and why you have certain boundaries. Instead of saying, "You're always taking up my time," you could say, "I need some time to work on my own projects, so I won't be able to make it to every family gathering."

Setting limits can mean being firm at times, especially if family members don't want to follow them or don't care about what you need. This could mean cutting down on the number of visits or calls, saying "no" to some requests, or even taking a break from some family activities for a while to focus on your own health. Even though these things can be hard to do, they are sometimes needed to make things better.

Plus, it's important to know that setting limits is an ongoing process, not a one-time thing. When your relationships and life changes, you may need to change your boundaries. Regularly check in with yourself to see if your boundaries are still meeting your needs and if they are being respected. If you need to, go over these rules again with your family to make sure they are still clear and effective.

Another important part of setting healthy limits with family members is being aware of and respecting their limits. They have the right to set limits, just like you do. Respecting each other is very important for keeping family relationships healthy and strong. Encourage people to talk about their boundaries openly, and be ready to listen and change how you act if necessary.

Last but not least, it's important to take setting boundaries with kindness and understanding. Family members might not always respect your boundaries, especially if they are used to interacting with you in a certain way. It's important to be patient and know that it can take time for family dynamics to change. As long as you are firm but kind, you can help your family understand how important boundaries are and work toward better, healthier relationships.

If you want to keep your emotional and mental health, you need to set healthy boundaries with your family. You can make your relationship with your family more balanced and satisfying by figuring out what needs to change, being clear about your boundaries, and going into the process with kindness and respect.

Making Family Traditions and Doing Things Together

Family activities and traditions are very important for making memories that will last a lifetime and strengthening the bonds between family members. Family traditions and shared experiences can be what keeps the generations together by giving them a sense of continuity, comfort, and who they are. When you have a larger group of friends, family traditions can also help you have a balanced and fulfilling social life by strengthening the relationships that shape your values and sense of belonging.

Making traditions that mean a lot to your family takes planning and creativity. When starting these traditions, it's important to think about what your family likes, what they believe in, and their cultural background. For example, if education and learning are important to your family, you could make it a habit to read books together and talk about them when you get together with your family. If you and your family like being outside, you could make going camping once a year a tradition. The important thing is to pick activities that are meaningful to your family as a whole and that everyone is excited to do.

Traditions in the family don't have to be hard to do or take a lot of time. Doing simple, everyday things can be just as meaningful. One way to encourage open communication and strengthen emotional bonds is to have a family dinner once a week where everyone is welcome to share their thoughts and experiences. Similarly, having a movie night once a month where everyone in the family picks the movie can help everyone enjoy the time together and respect each other's choices.

Along with regular traditions, it's important to plan unique activities that bring people together for holidays, birthdays, and family reunions. People can celebrate important moments, think about the past, and look forward to the future at these events. Aside from that, they help keep family values strong and pass on traditions to younger generations. A family might have a tradition of getting together to decorate the house for the holidays, with each person doing their own thing. In addition to making memories that will last a lifetime, these activities help the family feel like they belong and are proud of their achievements.

Making sure that family traditions are open to everyone and can be changed is another important part of making them. It's important to be flexible and meet the different wants and needs of everyone in the family as they grow and change. This could mean changing traditions to include new family members, like in-laws or stepchildren, or adapting activities to fit changes in health or mobility. Inclusivity makes sure that everyone, no matter what their situation is, feels valued and connected.

Also, it's important to remember that not all family traditions come from past generations; some can be made up from scratch. In fact, making new traditions can be a great way for families to bond and get to know each other better. For example, a family could make it a tradition to volunteer together over the holidays, which would teach the values of kindness and helping others. Adding new cultural elements to family traditions can also be a way to show how different family members' backgrounds and life experiences affect the traditions.

Planned activities are important, but unplanned times to bond are just as important. Often, the most meaningful interactions happen when you least expect them, like when you talk late at night, share a joke, or decide on the spot to go on a day trip. It's great to have regular traditions, but it's also important to be open to these random moments of connection, which can strengthen bonds in ways you wouldn't expect.

Making family traditions and doing activities together is important for keeping family relationships strong and healthy. You can help your family feel like they belong and are part of something bigger by planning the activities you do, making sure they are open to everyone, and being ready for spontaneous moments of connection. These traditions not only make family relationships stronger, but they also help you have a balanced and satisfying social life by supporting the relationships that shape your identity and values.

5 Things to Consider

Balancing Family and Other Relationships: Reflect on how you allocate time and energy between your family and other social connections. Consider whether you are maintaining a healthy balance that allows you to nurture all important relationships in your life without neglecting any.

Setting and Respecting Boundaries: Establishing clear boundaries with family members is crucial for maintaining your emotional and mental well-being. Consider how you can communicate your needs assertively while also respecting the boundaries of others in your family.

Cultural and Personal Expectations: Family expectations, shaped by cultural and personal values, can influence your social interactions and relationships. Reflect on how these expectations impact your decisions and whether they align with your own values and goals.

Creating Meaningful Family Traditions: Traditions and bonding activities are essential for fostering unity and creating lasting memories within your family. Think about how you can create or adapt family traditions that reflect your collective identity and values, ensuring they are inclusive and adaptable over time.

Navigating Overlapping Relationships: Introducing friends or romantic partners to your family can create cohesion but also potential conflicts. Consider how you manage these overlaps and ensure that all parties feel respected and valued, maintaining harmony across different social circles.

Reflection Questions

How do I currently balance my time and energy between family and other social relationships, and is this balance aligned with my personal values and priorities?

What boundaries do I need to establish or reinforce with my family members to protect my well-being, and how can I communicate these boundaries effectively and respectfully?

How do cultural and familial expectations influence my decisions and relationships, and are these influences in harmony with my own beliefs and goals?

What family traditions or bonding activities have been most meaningful to me, and how can I contribute to creating or sustaining traditions that foster a sense of belonging and unity?

How do I navigate the introduction and integration of friends or romantic partners into my family circle, and what steps can I take to ensure that these relationships coexist harmoniously?

Chapter 12

Recognizing When to Expand Your Circle

"The key is to keep company only with people who uplift you, whose presence calls forth your best."
Epictetus

Figuring out when to add new people to your social circle is a complicated process that requires you to look at how your current relationships are working and understand your own needs for growth and connection. As people's lives and priorities change, their social circles change, too. They can be small and close, or big and spread out. The choice to make new connections is often the result of a lot of different factors, including personal reflection, outside influences, and changing stages of life.

The first thing you should do to figure out if you need new connections is to look at your current social network. Think about whether the relationships you already have give you the support, fun, and variety you need. Having feelings of loneliness, being stuck, or being unhappy with your social interactions? If so, these feelings may mean you need to make new connections that give you new ideas, chances, and people to lean on.

Another thing to think about is how well your circle of relationships is balanced between different types of relationships. Are there parts of your life, like your job, hobbies, or personal growth, that your current network doesn't cover well enough? For example, if you just recently switched careers or found new interests, you may find that your old connections don't fit with what you want to do now. When this happens, adding people to your circle who share your new interests or professional goals can help you and give you unique perspectives.

The way things work in your current group of friends can also affect your choice to make new friends. Think about whether the interactions in your relationships are healthy and helpful, or whether there are patterns of negativity, conflict, or imbalance. If the relationships in your circle are unhealthy or don't give you many chances to grow, you might want to look for new connections that will make your social life better.

When deciding if you need new connections, personal growth and development are very important. People's needs and goals can change over time, which may mean they need to grow their social network. For instance, if you are starting a new phase in your life, like going to college, moving to a new city, or starting a new job, you might need to find connections that are compatible with these new challenges and experiences.

Also, keep in mind that adding new people to your circle doesn't mean getting rid of the ones you already have; it can just make them better. Making new friends can give you more support, new ideas, and a wider range of people to talk to. It can improve your social life without taking away from the value of the relationships you already have.

Figuring out if you need new connections means carefully looking at your current social situation, your personal growth, and the balance between the different kinds of relationships you have. You can make smart choices about when and how to grow your social circle in a way that benefits your health and personal growth by thinking about these things.

Looking for Different People in Social Networks

For a well-rounded and enjoyable social life, it's important to seek out different kinds of people in your social network. Diverse social connections, including people from different backgrounds, points of view, and life experiences, can lead to more insights, support, and chances. This diversity isn't just about making more connections; it's also about building relationships with people who bring new ideas and experiences to your social circle.

There are many benefits to having a diverse social network. Being exposed to different points of view can help you learn more about other cultures, values, and experiences. This broader view can help you grow as a person, understand other people better, and see the world in a more complex way. For example, interacting with people from different cultures can help you question what you think you know about other cultures and broaden your view of the world.

Diverse social networks can also help you in many areas of your life and give you useful tools and support. Different connections can give you advice, guidance, and chances that you might not be able to get in a group of people who are more like you. Connecting with professionals from different industries or backgrounds can give you unique insights and open doors to opportunities you might not have seen otherwise, for example if you are looking for a new career path.

To add more variety to your social network, start by thinking about the places where the people you already know might be lacking in variety. Check to see if there are any ideas, experiences, or interests that aren't well-represented in your network. Being aware of yourself can help you connect with people who have different experiences and points of view.

Joining activities or groups that put you in touch with new people is a good way to broaden your social network. This could mean joining clubs, going to events, or taking part in community activities that bring together people from different backgrounds. Volunteering for groups with different goals or causes can also help you meet people with different experiences and points of view.

You can also find different kinds of people to connect with at networking events and professional groups. Getting to know people from different roles, industries, or sectors can help you grow your professional network and give you new ideas that can help your career.

To find diversity, it's best to go into new relationships with an open mind and a sincere desire to learn from others. Having a more meaningful and enriching social experience can come from building relationships based on mutual respect and interest. By avoiding assumptions and stereotypes, you can interact with people as unique and valuable members of your network.

Looking for diversity in your social network makes your social life better by giving you a wider range of support and opportunities. Being open to new experiences and actively interacting with people from different backgrounds can help you grow as a person and make your social circle more welcoming and helpful.

Adding New People to Your Circle

If you want to make sure that adding new people to your social circle goes smoothly and positively, you need to give it some thought and manage it carefully. This process includes figuring out how to handle the interactions between current and new members, encouraging interactions that are open to everyone, and making connections that matter.

When adding new people to your social circle, you should think about how the group works and who is in it. Check to see how the new people will fit in with the current social scene and if there are any problems or conflicts that could arise. For instance, if the new member has similar interests or backgrounds to other members, this can make the process of integrating them go more smoothly. When there are big differences, on the other hand, it's important to handle them with openness and sensitivity.

When adding new members, communication is very important. Making it clear what the introduction is for and what is expected can help set a good mood. For example, if you are adding a new friend to a group of longtime friends, you should explain the situation and point out any shared interests or qualities that make the new friend a good fit for the group. This makes the group feel more open and helps current members see how valuable the new connection is.

For integration to go well, it's important to give new members chances to interact with the existing group. Set up activities, events, or gatherings where new members can meet and talk to other people in the circle. This gives people a chance to meet each other naturally and get to know each other better. A casual social event or a group project, for instance, can help people connect in a meaningful way and make new members feel more at ease and involved.

In addition, it's important to pay attention to what both new and old members have to say. Pay attention to any signs of stress or discomfort and do something about them. When there are problems or disagreements, you should be open and ready to find common ground. Making sure that everyone feels heard and important is an important part of keeping a positive and helpful social environment.

Accepting new people into your circle also means recognizing and appreciating the unique things they bring to the group. Get the people who are already in the group to value the new ideas and experiences that the new people bring to it. This openness makes the group more interesting and dynamic, and it makes new people feel welcome and valued.

The last thing to keep in mind is the speed of integration. Let new members get to know the group at their own pace, without pushing them or expecting them to make connections right away. It takes time to build meaningful relationships, and letting this process happen naturally leads to a better and longer-lasting integration.

Adding new people to your social circle requires clear communication, careful thought about how things are already going, and making time for meaningful interactions. By being careful with the integration process and encouraging acceptance, you can successfully grow your social circle and make the whole social experience better for everyone.

5 Things to Consider

Evaluating Current Social Dynamics: Reflect on the current state of your social circle and assess whether it meets your needs for support, engagement, and personal growth. Consider if there are gaps or areas where additional connections could enhance your overall social experience.

Identifying Areas for Growth: Determine whether your existing network aligns with your evolving interests, goals, or life changes. Seek new connections that complement these areas, such as professional aspirations, personal hobbies, or new life stages, to enrich and expand your social circle.

Understanding the Benefits of Diversity: Recognize the value of diversifying your social network. Diverse connections can provide different perspectives, broaden your worldview, and offer varied support and opportunities. Consider how incorporating individuals from different backgrounds and experiences can enhance your social and personal development.

Managing Integration Smoothly: When introducing new members to your circle, consider the existing dynamics and relationships. Plan the integration process carefully to foster positive interactions and minimize potential conflicts. Create opportunities for new and existing members to connect and build relationships organically.

Being Open to Spontaneous Connections: While planned expansions and introductions are important, remain open to spontaneous connections that arise naturally. Sometimes, unexpected interactions can lead to meaningful relationships and enrich your social circle in ways you might not have anticipated.

Reflection Questions

What gaps or limitations do I perceive in my current social circle, and how might expanding my network address these areas of need or dissatisfaction?

How have my interests, goals, or life circumstances evolved recently, and what types of new connections could support or align with these changes?

In what ways could increasing diversity in my social network enhance my personal growth and perspective, and how can I actively seek out and welcome such diversity?

How can I manage the process of introducing new members to my existing social circle to ensure a positive and inclusive integration? What strategies can I use to foster meaningful interactions between new and current members?

How can I stay open to and recognize spontaneous opportunities for new connections, and what steps can I take to cultivate these unexpected interactions into meaningful relationships?

Chapter 13

Sustaining Your Social Circle Over Time

"Friendship improves happiness and abates misery, by the doubling of our joy and the dividing of our grief."
Marcus Tullius Cicero

To keep a social circle going over time, you have to keep working at nurturing and maintaining relationships. Checking in with your connections on a regular basis is one of the best ways to do this. Check-ins at regular intervals are the building blocks of stronger relationships. They keep bonds strong and relevant even as life's demands change.

Checking in on a regular basis is more than just talking once in a while; it's an active way to stay involved and fill in any gaps in your relationships. This can be done in a number of ways, such as by setting up catch-up calls, sending thoughtful messages, or meeting in person. You can change how often and what these check-ins look like based on the type of relationship and the practicalities of your life.

Regular check-ins are important because they show that you care and are paying attention. As our lives get busier, it's easy for relationships to drift if we only talk to each other when we feel like it. Setting up a regular time to connect with people shows that you value and care about these relationships, which builds a sense of stability and dependability. Making this kind of conscious effort lowers the risk of social isolation and keeps connections alive and important.

Also, checking in on a regular basis lets you know what's going on in each other's lives and lets you celebrate successes and offer support during hard times. They help you clear up any problems or misunderstandings that come up, which builds trust and communication. A simple message asking about a friend's new job or a follow-up after an experience you both had can show that you are interested in the relationship and are committed to it.

Not only do regular check-ins help you keep up with individual relationships, they also help the health of your social circle as a whole. They help keep the group together and make it easier for people to talk to each other. For instance, planning regular get-togethers or group activities can help everyone get closer and keep the social life going strong.

Regular check-ins show how much work and intention you put into keeping your social circle strong. They show how important your relationships are to you and how determined you are to keep them strong over time. By making this a regular habit, you can keep your social connections strong and fulfilling, which will help you build a balanced and helpful social network.

Getting Used to Changes and Transitions in Life

Life is always changing and moving forward, and being able to handle these changes well is important for keeping friends. As you go through different stages of life, like changing jobs, moving, or reaching important personal milestones, you need to change how you keep and build your social connections.

To adapt to changes in your life, you need to be aware that your social needs and relationships may change as a result. For instance, if you move to a new city, you might have to start over with your social network. In this situation, it's important to go out of your way to make new connections and keep in touch with people you already know, even if they live far away.

One way to deal with this change is to be open and flexible in how you interact with other people. You should be ready to change how you interact with other people as your life changes. This could mean changing how you talk to people, like using digital tools to stay in touch with family and friends who live far away or discovering new ways to connect with people in your area, like coworkers and acquaintances.

Changes in your life can also happen in the people you hang out with. For instance, getting a new job or taking up a new hobby could help you meet people who share your interests. You can improve your social life and get more support during times of change by accepting these changes and adding new people to your network.

Keeping the lines of communication open and honest during changes is very important for keeping relationships strong. Tell your connections about your experiences and new information, and be honest about any problems you may be having. Being honest with others helps them understand and support you, which keeps your relationships strong during times of change.

During transitions, it's also important to be aware of and deal with any feelings of loss or disconnect that may come up. When people you know change, it can make you feel nostalgic or uncertain, and it's normal to be sad about the changes that happen. You can give your social network a sense of continuity and growth by being an active part of the adaptation process and looking for new ways to connect with other people.

Managing your social circle in a proactive and flexible way is important for adjusting to changes and transitions in your life. You can keep a supportive and active social network through different stages of life by being open to new connections, communicating clearly, and accepting that your relationships will change over time.

Making Your Connections More Valuable

To keep a meaningful and helpful group of friends, you need to remind your connections how important they are to you. As part of this process, you need to understand and affirm how important your relationships are, both to you and the people you interact with. You can help build a stronger and more fulfilling social network by showing how much you value your connections.

One way to keep your connections valuable is to show appreciation and gratitude for them on a regular basis. Simple actions, like thanking someone for their help or celebrating their accomplishments, can make your relationship stronger. These acts of thanks not only show that the relationship is important, but they also help create a positive and supportive social environment.

Along with verbal affirmations, it's also important to show that you value your connections through your actions. Being present and supportive during important times in other people's lives, like by helping them when they need it or going to important events with them, shows that you care about the relationship and are committed to it. These actions strengthen the bonds of friendship and support that make connections strong.

Putting time and effort into nurturing your relationships is another way to show how valuable your connections are. This means setting aside time for deep conversations, doing things together, and paying attention to each other's needs. Giving these parts of your relationships the attention they deserve will help them grow and last.

It's also important to deal with any problems or issues that come up in your social circle. To solve problems and keep relationships healthy, people need to be able to talk to each other in an open and helpful way. Dealing with problems head-on and working to find solutions shows that you value the connection by showing that you are willing to put effort into its resolution.

Lastly, thinking about how your connections have made your life better can help you see how valuable they are. Spend some time thinking about how your relationships affect your health, growth, and happiness in general. This reflection not only makes you value your connections more, but it also inspires you to keep caring for and maintaining them.

Boosting the worth of your connections means showing appreciation, putting effort into meaningful interactions, dealing with problems in a constructive way, and thinking about how your connections have made your life better. Doing these things regularly will help you build a strong and helpful group of friends that will make your life better and give you a sense of belonging and fulfillment.

5 Things to Consider

Commit to Regular Check-Ins: Regular communication is key to maintaining strong relationships. Consider how often you check in with your social circle and whether you could benefit from establishing a more consistent routine to keep connections vibrant and engaged.

Be Flexible During Life Transitions: Life changes are inevitable, and your social circle will need to adapt accordingly. Think about how you can remain open to new connections while also maintaining existing ones, especially during significant transitions like moving, changing jobs, or entering a new life stage.

Prioritize Open Communication: Clear and honest communication is essential for sustaining relationships over time. Reflect on how you communicate with your social circle, especially during conflicts or when life circumstances change, to ensure that your relationships remain strong and resilient.

Demonstrate the Value of Your Connections: Actions often speak louder than words. Consider how you show appreciation for your relationships, whether through gestures of gratitude, being present for important moments, or simply making time for those you care about.

Reflect on the Impact of Your Relationships: Take time to consider how your social circle contributes to your personal growth, happiness, and overall well-being. This reflection can help you recognize the importance of sustaining these connections and motivate you to continue nurturing them.

Reflection Questions

How often do I check in with the people in my social circle, and what impact does this frequency have on the strength of my relationships?

How well do I adapt my social connections during times of significant life changes, and what steps can I take to ensure my relationships remain strong during these transitions?

In what ways do I show appreciation and reinforce the value of my relationships? Are there additional actions I could take to better demonstrate my commitment to these connections?

When conflicts or misunderstandings arise within my social circle, how effectively do I communicate and work towards resolution? What could I improve in my approach to handling these situations?

How do my relationships contribute to my overall well-being and personal growth, and how can I continue to nurture these connections to sustain their positive impact on my life?

Chapter 14

Reflecting on Your Social Circle Journey

"Man's best support is a very dear friend."
Marcus Tullius Cicero

Building and maintaining a meaningful social circle is an ongoing process that is marked by constant growth and change. It's important to think back on this journey because it helps us celebrate the progress we've made, see how we and our relationships have changed, and value the variety of our social experiences.

To celebrate progress and growth, we need to remember the big and small events that have shaped how we interact with each other over time. Some examples of these milestones are deepening a friendship, ending a long-running argument, or making new friends who have made our lives better. Each of these events is a step forward in the ongoing process of social development, making the social network stronger and more fulfilling.

Thinking about how we've grown also helps us value how our social skills and emotional intelligence have changed over time. As time goes on, we get better at navigating the complicated world of social interactions. We learn how to handle conflicts better and become more sensitive to the wants and needs of others. Even though this development doesn't always happen in a straight line, it shows how well we can learn and change in social settings.

Also, part of celebrating growth is noticing how the people in our social circle have changed over time. Some relationships naturally get stronger over time, while others may fade or change into new types of connections. It shows that you are mature and emotionally strong when you can accept these changes as a normal part of social life. It shows that we know that the quality of our relationships is more important than the number of them, and that growing sometimes means letting go as well as holding on.

When we celebrate progress, it's important to remember that we play a part in making society better. We can be proud of our efforts to build and keep meaningful relationships by thinking about the ways we have contributed to the well-being of our social circle, whether it was through acts of kindness, support during hard times, or just being there for them all the time.

But celebrating growth isn't just about looking at ourselves; it's also about showing appreciation for the people who have helped us along the way. We can strengthen the bonds in our social circle even more by recognizing the contributions of others, the shared experiences that have brought us closer, and the accomplishments we share as a group. This practice strengthens the friendship and support that are necessary for relationships to last a long time.

In the end, celebrating progress and growth is a powerful way to remember how important our friends and family are. It shows how important it is to keep these connections strong, even when things change in your life. We become more grateful for the relationships that make our lives better and help us feel like we belong and are healthy when we take the time to think about how far we've come.

Learning from Problems and Mistakes

There will be problems along the way on any social journey, and it's important to think about the mistakes and problems you've had in order to keep growing. These problems, whether they're caused by misunderstandings, fights, or just the complicated nature of relationships, teach us important lessons that can help us interact better in the future.

To learn from our mistakes, we have to be ready to face hard truths about ourselves and how we act. Realizing the effects of our actions (or lack of actions) on others and being aware of how we may have caused problems or misunderstandings is part of it. Thinking about ourselves doesn't mean blaming ourselves. Instead, it means becoming more aware of our behavior patterns and how they affect how we interact with others.

One of the most important things you can learn from mistakes is how important it is to talk to people. A lot of social problems happen because people don't understand each other or talk clearly. By thinking about times when we didn't communicate well in the past, we can figure out how to better state our needs, listen to others, and handle tough conversations. Now that we know this, we can avoid making the same mistakes again and build relationships that are more open and honest.

Another thing that challenges often teach us is how important it is to set limits. Thinking about times in the past when boundaries were either too strict or too lax can help us figure out how to set and keep healthy boundaries in our relationships. To keep social interactions fair and balanced, we need to learn how to stand up for our own needs while also respecting the boundaries of others.

Problems also teach us a lot about how important it is to forgive others and ourselves. Keeping grudges or unresolved disagreements can hurt your relationships and stop you from growing as a person. We can let go of the emotional weight of past conflicts and start to heal and get along with others by thinking about them and working to forgive. This process not only fixes relationships, but it also makes people feel calm and strong.

Also, it's important to know that some problems may mean that you need to look at some relationships again. Some connections aren't meant to last, and over time they may become unhealthy or impossible to keep up. By thinking about these situations, we can decide which relationships are worth investing in and which ones are better off without us. This kind of discernment is necessary to keep a healthy and helpful group of friends.

To sum up, making mistakes and facing challenges is an important part of the social journey. To do this, you have to look at yourself, talk to others, set limits, forgive, and sometimes let go. By learning these lessons, we give ourselves the tools we need to deal with other people more wisely and kindly in the future.

Making Plans for the Future

It's important to look ahead and make plans for the future as we think about our social circle journey. When we set intentions, we think about the kinds of social relationships we want to build, the habits and behaviors we want to pick up, and the social goals we want to reach.

Before we can set intentions, we need to know what we value most in relationships. Finding these core elements—whether they're trust, loyalty, mutual support, or shared values—helps us decide what to do and how to act in the future. When we make sure that our social interactions are in line with our values, we build a more genuine and satisfying group of friends who reflect who we really are.

You can also set intentions around specific goals or areas that you want to get better at. One example of an intention could be to practice more active listening or to be more honest with others if we know that communication is an area where we need to work on. If we know we need to set better boundaries, we might promise to be more clear and polite about what we need in the future. These intentions help us build stronger and healthier relationships by setting rules for how we should act and talk to each other.

Making a promise to keep learning and growing is another important part of setting intentions. Relationships with other people are always changing, and there is always room for growth and improvement. We make sure that our social circle stays alive and changing by committing to being open to feedback, improving our people skills all the time, and looking for new experiences and connections.

When we set intentions, we also think about how our social circle will change in the future. This could mean thinking about what new connections we want to make, how we can strengthen existing ones, or how we will keep in touch with our friends as our lives change in the future. It is possible to make sure that our social circle continues to meet our needs and help us grow if we think about the future.

Lastly, it's important to remember that setting intentions doesn't mean sticking to a strict plan. Instead, it means deciding on a direction and being open to different ways to reach our goals. Social relationships are complicated and hard to plan for. To keep a healthy and fulfilling social circle, we need to be able to change our plans as things happen.

Setting goals for the future is an important part of thinking about our social circle journey. It means making sure that our interactions with others are in line with our values, setting clear goals for improvement, committing to ongoing growth, picturing the future of our relationships, and being open to changing how we do things. We make sure that our social circle keeps growing in a way that makes our lives better and helps our personal and social health by doing this.

5 Things to Consider

Acknowledge Your Growth: Take time to celebrate the progress you've made in building and maintaining your social circle. Recognize the milestones and achievements that have contributed to the depth and quality of your relationships.

Learn from Challenges: Reflect on the mistakes and difficulties you've encountered along the way. Consider how these experiences have shaped your understanding of relationships and what lessons you can carry forward to improve future interactions.

Value Communication: Effective communication is key to maintaining healthy relationships. Consider how you can enhance your communication skills, whether through active listening, clearer expression of your needs, or more constructive conflict resolution.

Set Clear Intentions: Think about the kind of relationships you want to cultivate moving forward. Set intentions that align with your values and goals, and be mindful of how your actions can support the growth and sustainability of your social circle.

Be Open to Change: Social circles are dynamic and evolving. Be prepared to adapt to changes in your relationships, whether they involve deepening connections, letting go of toxic ties, or welcoming new members into your circle. Flexibility and openness are essential for maintaining a healthy and fulfilling social life.

Reflection Questions

What are the key moments of growth and progress in your social circle journey, and how have they shaped your relationships?

What challenges or mistakes have you encountered in your social relationships, and what lessons have you learned from these experiences?

How effectively do you communicate within your social circle? In what areas could your communication improve to enhance your relationships?

What intentions can you set for the future of your social circle, and how do these intentions align with your personal values and goals?

How can you remain open and adaptable to changes in your social circle while continuing to nurture and sustain meaningful connections?

Chapter 15
Embracing the Power of Few

"Life is nothing without friendship."
Marcus Tullius Cicero

In a world where the number of connections is more important than the quality of those connections, the idea of embracing the power of few is very different from what most people think. Because of how connected we are now, many people think that having more friends is a sign of success and influence. But when we look deeper into how people connect with each other and the social interactions that happen, we find a different truth: the deepest and most important relationships are often the ones that are few but very deep.

The power of few is not about being alone or being exclusive. Instead, it's about being deliberate and smart about building relationships that matter. It's a recognition that energy, time, and emotional investment are limited resources. Focusing these on a small group of people greatly increases the chance of making connections that last. For the most part, the power of few means building a group of friends who share your values, goals, and true self.

This way of doing things does come with some problems. You have to be ready to say "no," set limits, and deal with the discomfort of possibly letting other people down. However, these challenges are necessary steps to make friends who will help and support you. When you accept the power of a few, you make room for real connection to grow, for trust and closeness to grow, and for mutual support and growth to become the foundations of your relationships.

The power of few also challenges the idea that having a lot of friends or followers is the best way to measure social capital. Instead, it says that real social capital comes from a few close relationships that are strong and real. These are the ties that make you feel like you belong, help you understand, and give you support through good times and bad. These are the kinds of relationships that make a big difference in our emotional health and personal growth.

We are always thinking about how to improve ourselves when we accept the power of a few. This means that we should regularly look at our social circle, pay attention to who takes up our time and space, and make changes as needed to make sure that our relationships stay in line with our values and goals. Being self-aware and dedicated to nurturing the connections that matter most are both important for this practice, which is always changing.

Last Words on Taking Care of Your Friends and Family

It becomes clear that building a small but strong group of friends is both an art and a science as we think about the process. It takes a careful balance of emotional intelligence, purpose, and strength. Taking care of your social circle isn't something you do passively; it's something you do on a regular basis to build relationships that are good for both of you.

At the heart of this process of nurturing is the idea that relationships are living things that change, grow, and sometimes need to be pruned. Just like a gardener carefully chooses which plants to grow, you need to be aware of who you let into your inner circle and how you invest in those relationships in order to nurture your social circle. In this case, you might have to let go of relationships that aren't good for you or work to strengthen relationships with people whose values and goals are similar to your own.

It's also important to understand that relationships work both ways. Forging strong relationships with other people means not only asking for help and support, but also giving it in return. This kind of giving and taking is what builds trust and closeness, and it's how relationships get stronger and last longer across time.

Communication is a very important part of keeping up with people in your social circle. Any healthy relationship needs to be able to talk to each other in an open, honest, and caring way. Misunderstandings can be cleared up, trust can be built, and emotional bonds can grow stronger through communication. So, learning how to communicate well, like how to actively listen, make your needs and boundaries clear, and handle conflicts in a healthy way, is important for the health and longevity of your social circle.

Building up shared experiences and rituals is another important part of taking care of your social circle. These give people in the group a sense of continuity and belonging. Whether it's regular get-togethers, hobbies you share, or even simple traditions like celebrating life milestones together, these things help to strengthen the bonds between people and make memories that last, which makes your social circle stronger.

Moving Forward with Goals and Intentions

It is important to approach your social life with intention as you move forward. This means that you should be intentional about the connections you make and the relationships you keep alive. Making a promise to align your social interactions with your values, goals, and overall health is part of it.

To move forward with purpose, you need to be aware of yourself and think about what you want. To do this, you need to ask yourself important questions about the relationships you want to build and the part you want them to play in your life. Do your current relationships help you grow as a person and be happy? Do they fit with your needs and goals? Are there places where you need to change things or set limits?

Being aware of how you spend your time and energy is another part of purposeful social engagement. It's easy to feel overwhelmed by all the social interactions in a world that is always trying to get our attention. You can have a more balanced and satisfying social life, though, if you put quality over quantity and give priority to the relationships that really matter.

Also, moving forward with purpose and intention means being open to new ideas and accepting change. People in our social circles change as we do as we grow and change. To do this, you need to be open to new people and opportunities and ready to let go of relationships that aren't giving you anything good. The trick is to find the right balance between holding on to the important things and making room for new relationships and experiences.

As you continue to build and keep up your social circle, keep in mind that this is not a journey to perfection, but one to progress. It means learning new things, changing things, and getting better at making and keeping meaningful connections. You can make your social life not only fulfilling but also very good for your overall health and sense of self by focusing on the power of a few close friends, taking care of your social circle, and moving forward with purpose.

In conclusion, one of the best parts of life is the process of making and keeping a small but meaningful group of friends. Taking care of the relationships that really matter takes time, work, and a promise to do so. But the benefits—like deep connections, support for each other, and personal growth—are well worth the time and effort. I hope you find happiness and fulfillment on this path. May the power of a few and the strength of your social circle guide you.

5 Things to Consider

Quality Over Quantity: Reflect on the value of maintaining a small, close-knit social circle. Consider how focusing on a few meaningful relationships can lead to deeper connections and greater emotional support compared to a large, superficial network.

Intentional Relationship Building: Think about the importance of being intentional in the relationships you cultivate. Are your current connections aligned with your values and goals? Are you investing your time and energy in relationships that genuinely enrich your life?

Continuous Reflection and Adjustment: Understand that social circles are dynamic. Regularly assess your relationships and be open to making changes, whether that means strengthening certain bonds, setting boundaries, or letting go of connections that no longer serve you.

The Role of Communication: Consider the critical role that effective communication plays in nurturing your social circle. Reflect on how you can improve your communication skills to foster trust, resolve conflicts, and deepen your connections.

Moving Forward with Purpose: Think about how you can approach your social life with greater intention and purpose. Whether it's being open to new relationships or refining existing ones, make choices that align with your personal growth and overall well-being.

Reflection Questions

How have your closest relationships shaped your personal growth, and what steps can you take to continue nurturing these connections?

In what ways have you been intentional about the relationships you cultivate, and how can you ensure that your social circle continues to align with your values and goals?

How do you balance the need for connection with the need for boundaries in your relationships? Are there areas where you need to make adjustments?

What communication habits do you currently practice within your social circle, and how might improving these skills enhance the depth and quality of your relationships?

As you move forward, what intentions will you set for your social life, and how will you ensure that your relationships remain a source of support and fulfillment?

Further Reading

"Meditations" by Marcus Aurelius

"Letters from a Stoic" by Seneca

"Discourses and Selected Writings" by Epictetus

"Cicero: Selected Works" by Cicero

"Unbothered: How to Not Let the Little Things in Life Get to You" by John Morrison

"The Socratic Life: An Argument to Lead an Examined Life" by John Morrison

"Choose Coffee: How to Live in an Increasingly Nihilistic World" by John Morrison

www.ingramcontent.com/pod-product-compliance
Lightning Source LLC
La Vergne TN
LVHW100325210926
848480LV00003B/1257
* 9 7 9 8 3 4 9 4 0 5 1 3 6 *